WRITING AND ILLUSTRATING
CHILDREN'S BOOKS

PUBLICATION

Two Perspectives

by **Berthe Amoss** *and* **Eric Suben**

WRITER'S DIGEST BOOKS
Cincinnati, Ohio

Writing and Illustrating Children's Books for Publication — Two Perspectives.
Copyright © 1995 by Berthe Amoss and Eric Suben
Printed in China by More Than A Card, Inc.

Published by Writer's Digest Books, an imprint of F&W Publications, Inc., 1507 Dana Avenue, Cincinnati, Ohio, 45207.
1-800-289-0963.
Sixth edition.

Library of Congress Catalog-in-Publication Data

Amoss, Berthe.
    Writing and illustrating children's books for publication : two
perspectives / by Berthe Amoss and Eric Suben. -- 1st ed.
        p. cm.
    Includes index.
    ISBN 0-89879-722-5 (alk. paper)
    1. Children's literature--Authorship. 2. Illustration of books.
I. Suben, Eric. II. Title.
PN147.5.A48 1995   95-17164
808. 06'8--dc20   CIP

This hardcover edition of *Writing and Illustrating Children's Books for Publication* features a "self jacket" that eliminates the need for a separate dust jacket. It provides sturdy protection for your book while it saves paper, trees and energy.

The authors and publisher have made every effort to trace the ownership of all copyrighted material reproduced in this book. They now acknowledge and thank the following individuals and entities for permission to use such material:

Scholastic, Inc.
Western Publishing Company, Inc.
Hyperion Books for Children
UFS, Inc.
The New Yorker Magazine, Inc.
The Times-Picayune
Harper & Row
Jennifer Rosen
Patsy H. Perritt
Auseklis Ozols
Jean Cassells
Emily Arnold McCully
Joan Elizabeth Goodman
Kathy Allert
Amye Rosenberg
Susan Larson
Elizabeth Gordon
Eden Ross Lipson
Mary Price Robinson
Coleen Salley
Matt Berman
Richard Peck
Meb Norton
Marigny Dupuy
Elizabeth Robeau Amoss
Kevin McCaffrey

Any use of copyrighted material without permission is the result of inadvertence or mistake and will be corrected in future printings after written notice to the publisher.

Dedicated to the memory of Doris Duenewald — ES
Dedicated to the memory of Ursula Nordstrom — BMA

Edited by Jack Heffron
Written by Berthe Amoss and Eric Suben
Interior design by Rebecca Blake
Cover design by Rebecca Blake
Cover illustrations by Berthe Amoss

Table of Contents

Introduction

ABOUT THE AUTHORS

Berthe Amoss and Eric Suben have taught a large number of classes and workshops and have appeared at a variety of conferences, including the Deep South and New Orleans Writers conferences. They call their presentation "Two Perspectives" because their backgrounds give them different points of view on the most important skills needed for the person interested in writing children's books: writing the books and selling them to publishers.

Most courses or manuals about writing for children focus on the writing, but writing successfully may hinge on understanding the realities of the publishing marketplace. What is written must be salable to publishers or the message will not reach children.

Berthe (pronounced *bear-t*) is the author and/or illustrator of numerous picture books and young-adult novels. She taught children's literature at Tulane University for twelve years, during which time she also wrote a column on children's books for *The Times-Picayune*. She is in charge of product development for More Than A Card, Inc., a card and book publishing company.

Eric, now a practicing attorney, was formerly editor-in-chief of

Golden Books and a director of the Children's Book Council. He has been a frequent panelist and lecturer on children's publishing, has written articles on the subject, and is the author of more than twenty-five picture books for young children.

In preparation for writing this work, the authors have collaborated in teaching courses at Tulane and a series of day-long workshops. Their advice comes from extensive professional experience, intensive work with students, and familiarity with the issues of greatest concern to students. The unique writing and illustrating exercises presented in this book were developed for these classes and workshops. Students and workshop participants at all levels have used the exercises to draw insights into their own work and help build needed skills.

Berthe and Eric use the "case-history" method to teach valuable lessons. Berthe, the daughter of an attorney and law professor, and Eric, a lawyer, are familiar with this technique used in American law schools in which students read accounts of actual cases and must infer general rules of law from these accounts. Similarly, the authors have peppered this book with stories from their actual experiences as a way of imparting useful principles for writers.

One of the stimulating aspects of *Two Perspectives* is that the authors do not always agree with each other. Often, their knowledge overlaps, but just as often one view enlightens the other. But Berthe and Eric do agree about the basics: starting with clear, correct prose that is lively and expressive; staying in touch with "the child within"; and writing from your passion. This book is the product of their shared love for good children's books and the desire to share their enthusiasm with you.

— Jack Heffron
Editor, Writer's Digest Books

Chapter 1

PROMISES

---

*I*f you want to write for children, your biggest problem may be finding time. You have a demanding job in an office or small children at home or both of the above and then some. Perhaps you're not sure you have talent or if your idea is right or if you should do your own illustrations.

Maybe you've already written something and want to get it published but don't know how to go about it. Should you get an agent, and if so, how? You've heard of books that were accepted "over the transom," as the saying goes; will someone read your manuscript if you just mail it to a publisher? And what about mailing it to more than one publisher at a time?

And then, there's the greatest mystery of all: What are editors looking for? Ursula Nordstrom of Harper & Row, one of the most influential editors of children's books in our times, answered that question: "I don't know," she said, "but I recognize it when I see it."

This is our promise to you: If you read this book, using it to guide you as you write your own book for children, you will be able to produce a publishable manuscript, and you will understand the process of getting it published.

We believe this book is different from, and more helpful than, any other you may have read on the subject of writing and illustrating children's books. We believe this because of two unique concepts incorporated in the format: Our book gives you two perspectives, that of the editor and that of the creator, and it uses the case-history method to convey the information you need in order to be successful.

Two Perspectives is designed so that it can be used in different ways. There are ten chapters, eight of which have the following features: Advice, Case Histories, Exercises, Reading Lists, and Self-Editing Checklists. For easy reference, each part can be identified by its own logo.

ADVICE

This section of each chapter will explain as clearly as possible the main areas of concern and opportunities for development under each subject heading. Where possible, we attempt to give concrete examples and use graphic devices, such as charts, to impart information in a lucid, memorable way. The Advice sections of this book draw heavily from work with students and from our teaching experience.

CASE HISTORIES

The case histories are stories from our own actual experiences and from working with other authors, illustrators, and editors. Generally, the stories are dramatic illustrations of the points discussed in the text. Sometimes, however, a case history will show an instance where an exception to one of our "rules" was the right approach, and sometimes a case history will be included for the fun of showing the wacky things that happen in publishing. Because these stories are truly products of our different perspectives, we have identified each one with the name of whichever of us supplied the incident.

WRITING AND ILLUSTRATING EXERCISES

The exercises are included to help you build important skills discussed in the text. Doing the exercises should help you focus on the process of writing for children by concentrating your mind on the challenges and helping you build techniques for overcoming them. Sometimes we do not give an answer to an exercise because the goal is for you to find your own answer and in this way become more flexible in identifying different approaches to your writing and illustrating.

The exercises are designed to further your own story and to keep you writing every day, another important aspect of creating a successful book for children. The assignments pull together the threads developed by the chapter's exercises, and each is designed to have a practical result, such as writing down an idea, or writing a query letter, or making a book dummy or outline or doing your own illustrations.

READING LISTS

Reading is one of the most important things you can do if you want to write well. The lists have been prepared carefully with the help of teachers, booksellers, and librarians who know children and their literature. Listed are children's books as well as books written for adults with a strong interest in writing for children.

SELF-EDITING CHECKLISTS

These lists of questions and reminders provide guidelines for assessing the work you've done in your own story. The lists will help you polish your work so that it is as good as can be before you submit it to an editor. You will be able to view your work critically and anticipate what an editor would find wrong in your story.

Because an illustrator is involved, your work may not be finished until the book is on the press. The collaborative publishing process requires that you be flexible, cooperative, and willing to solve problems. Most important and often overlooked is the need to spell and use grammar correctly. Look for redundancies and gaps in logic, and fix them before an editor must. Submitting a clean, well-written, carefully edited manuscript gives you a far better chance of being read by a busy editor, who might be turned off by time-consuming sloppiness, no matter how much talent is hidden in the pages.

You can use *Two Perspectives* in different ways, depending on your personal goals. It can be used as a reference book, and you can dip into it as the need arises. We have also designed the book as an eight-lesson, self-taught course. Using this approach, the reader works through each chapter in order, doing the exercises, answering the questions, reading the suggested books, and working on his own story as he goes along.

By using the book in this manner, the reader can produce a publishable picture book manuscript in eight weeks, that is, one chapter per week. If you are writing a chapter book, you should be able to finish three polished chapters and an outline. You can, of course, extend the time spent on each of our eight "course" chapters, but we recommend as short a period as possible. Long-term commitments are difficult for most people, and we believe that it is crucial to complete a manuscript and actually send it off to a publisher.

If you take the course approach, you will find that the lessons work all together. (Chapters one and ten are intended to provoke your thinking and are not directed at building skills as the other eight chapters are.) As you grow more confident in your skills, you may do things in a different order or spend more time on one lesson. For now, separating the skills you need into discrete challenges is an organized way to learn and grow.

We can give you the tools to succeed, but you must learn to use them; the commitment and hard work must come from you.

THE FUNDAMENTALS: TWO R'S AND TWO W'S

There are some constants, things you should do continuously as you work your way through this book.

1) READ

Spend time in bookstores and libraries. Go through your children's or any children's bookshelves. Constant exposure to the vast range of material published for children can help you appreciate the wide variety of opportunities and possibilities in writing for children. It can also help you learn what is considered publishable.

Poking through bookstores doesn't require a great investment of money: Picture

books are short, and you can read several while you stand casually browsing through the children's shelves. The advantage to reading in a bookstore is that you can watch the reactions that children and parents have to books. Talk to the bookseller; most will be happy to share their observations with you. You can hear something about the reasons parents buy particular books. And you can see how books are merchandised, formatted, illustrated, positioned on shelves or in displays, hand sold by bookstore personnel.

Many children's books are sold because booksellers take time to "push" them to consumers. Listen to what booksellers say in recommending books. Ask them which books are selling best and why, which are their favorites and why. Remember that after you sell your book to a publisher, the publisher sells it to a bookseller. The bookseller is the first "consumer" of your book. If she doesn't like it, it will never get on the shelves and have the opportunity to appeal to parents and children. (On the other hand, remember, too, that one bookseller's opinion is only one bookseller's opinion.)

Follow the same line of questioning with children's librarians. Remember that their tastes tend to be more conservative — they're looking for redeeming value, not just fun, but they are the tastemakers in the field of children's books, the reviewers and award-givers. Traditionally, they also comprise one of the largest and most lucrative markets for children's books.

At the library, request and read the children's book reviews in *Publishers Weekly*, *School Library Journal*, *Voice of Youth Advocates*, *Horn Book*, and other publications. You'll find reviews of children's books in your local newspaper as well. Comb the reviews for glimmerings of ideas that you might like to handle. Find the books and read them. Try to find what the reviewer liked or didn't like about the book. Figure out how the author or illustrator did it.

2) REMEMBER

Think back to your own childhood, to the stories and books you liked best, the questions you wondered about most, the people, places, things, and experiences you liked best and least, and why. Think of situations you were in that revealed something about your inner thoughts and feelings, even though you may not have been aware of them at the time.

Remember that a tiny event from your childhood may have seemed like a great dramatic episode to you, and it may contain the germ of an idea to start you on a story. Your memory should become your greatest source of inspiration, not only for story ideas, but also for true feelings to express in your writing. Think about what happened to you at different times, but also about how it made you feel. Try to remember your interests at different ages. Try to remember what you were doing at the time

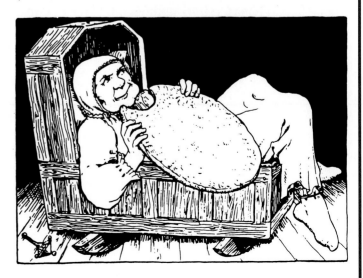

of those different experiences: Could you swim? Could you read? Could you ride a trike? A bike? Could you tie your own shoes? Remembering surrounding circumstances can help make the experience truthful in your writing. Try to picture the scenes you remember, and write down the details.

3) WATCH

Observe children at every opportunity — on city buses, at playgrounds, at parties. Be aware of their ages and the interests and skills they have developed. What are their motor skills? If you hear them say things that intrigue you, take notes and look for germs of ideas.

If you have or know school-age children, talk to teachers. What curriculum is your child learning this year? What skills does the teacher expect the children to master? Think of ways to work these concepts into stories — letters, numbers, colors, opposites, word recognition, addition and subtraction. What books does the teacher read to her classes? What is the classroom setting like? Are the children responsible for plants? Animals? What is the classroom routine?

If you have not watched children for a while, make the effort to observe them for what they wear, say, do. Watch children's television and movies. They can help you understand children's interests. They can instruct you in ways of expressing meaningful themes through colorful characters and action. Look for high-quality media presentations. The people who produce *Sesame Street* and the Disney movies know a great deal about educating, entertaining, and enriching children. You can learn a lot from their work.

Watch the world around you. What did you always want to know about that a child might like to know about, too? Why do animals do the things they do? Why is the sky blue?

In our workshops, we have noticed that participants who are around children (teachers, librarians, mothers) often begin with a very definite idea for a book based on a need they perceive. For example, the mother of a handicapped child might want to write a book that explains her child's handicap to other children so that her child will find acceptance and understanding among peers.

Or a librarian might want to write a book about a subject that he perceives is missing from library shelves but requested by children. Beverly Cleary, a librarian, wrote her classic *Ramona* because children kept asking for books about other children like themselves. Cleary's editor said, "I never edit Beverly's books; I only rearrange commas." Librarians know what children like, and they know how to write.

4) WRITE

The most important thing you can do is write. Keep a journal, and if you are writing a picture book, illustrate your journal with your own drawings. Even if you are not working on a story, write down your opinions of the books you read. Take notes on the children you watch. Put your memories into words. Writing is like any other skill, requiring constant exercise to improve. When you are not working on a manuscript, keep a written record of your thoughts, feelings, and observations that apply to children and children's books.

If you are working on a manuscript, do some writing on it every day — even a sentence or two can be constructive. The most important thing you can do in working on a story is to keep the ball rolling, to stay in the world of your story with the characters you've created. You may find a new and better way to express your ideas, a more accurate or appropriate description. A story is a living, growing thing: You are bringing the characters and situation to life through your words. Like other living things, your story requires attention and care. Take time to nurture it with new writing every day.

You may reach a point where you are frustrated with your story or have created a problem you don't know how to solve. Put it aside temporarily and start on something new. By facing a new set of challenges, you may find a way out of your problem in the first story while you are creating another manuscript. A dividend of this style of working may be that you end up with two good stories to sell rather than one. Although your aim should always be quality rather than quantity, remember that the more stories you write, the more opportunities you give yourself to be published.

In your writing, even in the journal you keep for yourself, be conscious of writing in the simplest, most direct language. Keep a dictionary and thesaurus close at hand, and make sure you are using and spelling any questionable words correctly. Keep a style guide, such as Strunk & White's *The Elements of Style*, at hand, and check your punctuation, capitalization, and usage. Words and punctuation are your tools, and you should be sure you are using them correctly. If you are, editors will love you, because you are saving them work.

Periodically read through your journal for thoughts or ideas you may have overlooked in thinking about stories to write. Go back to unfinished stories and try to finish them. Do not throw away any drafts or early stages of your manuscripts — as you write and revise, you may want to refer to them. Read your writing aloud. Read it to others whose opinion you trust, and listen to their criticism.

Our success is based primarily on luck and perseverance. We do believe that we have talent, but we also believe that if you yearn to write for children, you also have talent. The word *yearn* is the essence of talent. We believe that if you're persistent enough, the law of averages almost always catches up with you and you will get published. Feel the passion, have faith, and do the hard work. We've put our "two perspective" tools for your success into this book; it is our kept promise to you.

Chapter 2

THE CHILD WITHIN

IDEAS AND GETTING STARTED

ADVICE

*Y*ou may be reading this book with the idea that when you finish, you will begin to write your own book. If that is what you're doing, you've already put a "writer's block" in the middle of your path to success.

To take full advantage of *Two Perspectives*, you should make up your mind that you are going to write a book as you read and that when you have completed the book, you will have a finished manuscript to mail to a publisher. If you already have a finished manuscript, you should work on it as you progress through the book and mail it to a publisher after you have self-edited it on the basis of what you have learned from *Two Perspectives*.

Reading about writing but not actually writing on a regular basis gives you only the illusion of learning. Our advice to you (and we will say it over and over again because it is the most important thing of all) is this: Form the habit of writing every day, whether it is work on your manuscript or journal keeping.

This chapter is devoted to helping you organize and get started. The best way to do this is to find your special time and place, and set a goal. Plan to have a finished manuscript that you will mail to a publisher at the end of eight weeks.

But first, let us define clearly the categories of children's books in use throughout.

We can divide children's books into categories by age group, by subject matter, by genre, etc. But categories often overlap, and reading levels aren't always consistent with age levels. Also, the most successful books (e.g., E. B. White's *Charlotte's*

Web) defy labels and are just plain good literature.

For the purposes of this book, however, we will define the three broad categories we refer to most often:

PICTURE BOOK: a book for very young children in which the illustrations play a role as important as the text; for children approximately 2-6.

CHAPTER BOOK: a longer book for older children who are learning or have just learned to read, with more sophisticated subject matter, treatment, and language; for children approximately 6-10.

YOUNG ADULT (YA) NOVEL: within the novel category are two distinct subcategories, one for 10- to 12-year-olds and another for ages 12 and older which contain more mature subject matter and language suitable for young teens.

If you're writing a short picture book, eight weeks is long enough to make a "dummy," a handmade book with sketches, to submit to a publisher. If you're writing a chapter book or a YA, you can mail three polished chapters and an outline. Knowing that you will have a completed project at the end of eight weeks will motivate you to make a time commitment and postpone things that aren't absolutely necessary.

To help you find time, think of it this way: There are some things you must continue to do, but if you think about it, you will find that you are currently doing a lot of things that aren't really necessary; if you postpone or eliminate these things for just eight weeks, you can find two hours a day for your writing. If you're a night person, stay up after your house is quiet. If you think better in the morning, wake up early. If you work, use your lunch hour.

Choose a writing place and keep everything you need there, so that you won't waste time looking for a sharpened pencil or having to put paper in the word processor or

CASE HISTORY (BERTHE)

When my children were small, I got up at five every morning to write my first young adult novel, The Chalk Cross. *It was the only time of the day I could call my own, and I grew to love that special time with my characters, so much so that I still keep to my schedule. When I am all alone in the early morning, I really feel as though I have entered another world, the world of my characters.*

For me, there is something almost magic about the place I choose to do my work. It is a small room upstairs lined with books. It has a large casement window and a battered, upholstered chair, my girlhood desk, and my drawing table. Early in the morning, when I come into my room, once occupied by a small son, I open the window to a still-dark sky, and enter my fictional world.

The Chalk Cross *was set in 1840 in New Orleans, and I had to do a lot of research. I read in snatches of time, e.g., when the children napped or at play time while I sat with them. When I had to do finished watercolor illustrations for my first picture book, I hired a baby-sitter for three hours every afternoon.*

Writing Lost Magic, *set in medieval times, required even more research, but by the time I wrote it, just three years ago, my children were older and I could spend hours at the library or growing and studying medieval herb gardens, even visiting herb gardens in England, Connecticut, and the Cloisters in New York.*

printer when you have time to write.

A loose-leaf binder containing everything you need can go with you everywhere. Use indexed sections to organize and separate various parts or chapters of your writing, envelope dividers for material relating to your subject, and one plastic page with a zipper for pencils and a pencil sharpener.

Carry your binder in your briefcase if you go to work, or keep it at your writing place at home so that you can pick it up quickly if you have a moment and can't get to a word processor. Just eight weeks, remember!

Think one chapter at a time and a novel does not seem such a formidable task. It is said that Margaret Mitchell used that approach when she wrote *Gone With the Wind*, stacking each completed chapter in a pile behind her desk.

"Only connect" is a phrase out of E.M. Forster's *Howard's End*. It was used also by P.L. Travers, author of *Mary Poppins*, as her title for an essay on children's literature. Take it for your mantra, and connect everything you do so that all your activities relate to your writing.

By making everything you have to do relate to what you are writing and/or illustrating, you're really doing two things at once: saving time and creating an environment for developing ideas. You may think that your "real" job is totally unrelated to

writing children's books, but that's only because the idea of connecting is new to you. Try it and you'll see what we mean. "Only connect" is a kind of mind-set.

Finding ideas is easy if you're around children, but if you're not, take comfort from the fact that some of the best writers for children — such as Maurice Sendak, author of the classic *Where the Wild Things Are* — aren't either. Besides that's only one way to get ideas. The real trick is to change the phrase "looking for ideas" to "recognizing ideas," and you'll soon see that good material is all around you. If your mind is set and you are thinking "children's books," everything that happens during the day will suggest ideas to you.

Talent? It's buried in all of us; it just has to be nourished. As we said earlier, we believe that talent is composed of large quantities of yearning, hard work, a strong

desire to express yourself in writing or illustration, and a willingness to devote yourself to the task. If you examine the careers of published writers, you'll find that hard work, perseverance, and luck played major roles in their success. For now, the most important thing you can do is to get started with a goal in mind.

Read as many children's books as possible. Haunt the children's sections of bookstores and libraries. Talk to librarians and booksellers. Observe children's reactions to their books; they are the final judges of their own literature. No book ever became a classic if children did not love it. Read, write, and think children's books. If you do, you'll "recognize" your idea when you see it, and if you've organized your time, found your special place to work, and set a goal, you will be well on your way to success.

At the start, nothing is more important than remembering what it was like to be a child

Case History (Berthe)

When I'd finally written the picture-book story I knew worked, I very nearly didn't show it to an editor. I had an appointment in New York at Harper & Row, and I was nervous and early. I went into Doubleday's Fifth Avenue bookstore to browse. I can't remember the exact title of the children's book I saw that struck fear into my heart, but it's meaning suggested it was just like my manuscript, It's Not Your Birthday.

"It's already been written," I said aloud. But when I opened the book, it was entirely different from mine. Remember that everything has been written about before, but that if your approach to an idea is fresh and original, you will be writing from the inside out, and it will be your story.

— not the those-were-the-days kind of remembering, but recapturing how you felt and thought about the world around you, rediscovering the child within. Often that child-like point of view will surprise you because you have replaced it with something more appropriate to maturity. Would-be writers for children who are not in touch with the child within often write little sermons instead of stories; they are writing from an adult point of view, thinking they have to teach or preach to the little ones. Although every good book for children enriches the reader in some way, the message always emerges from the story in the form of its theme, never in a didactic way.

Journal writing is another way to reach the child within and to begin to see again the world from a child's point of view. An illustrated journal with sketches you've drawn is even better.

Don't say you can't draw. If you have trouble thinking of yourself as an artist, then think of yourself as a reporter and record in picture form what you see or whatever needs illustrating.

Here is my memory map of my bedroom in the house I lived in until I was 12, more than fifty years ago. Drawing it, I remembered forgotten incidents loaded with emotion and feeling I had then for people and things, a childlike view of the world.

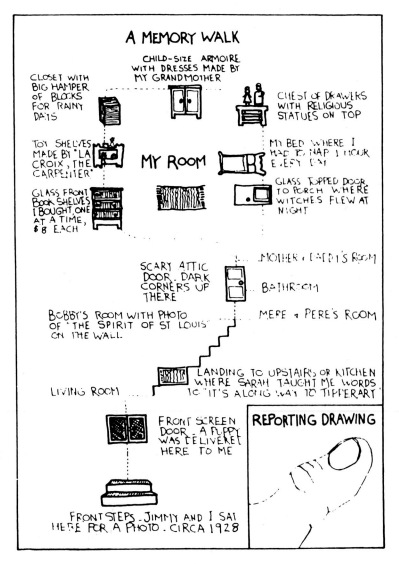

EXERCISE

1) Make a "reporter drawing" describing an object nearby.
2) Do a memory map of a place dear to you in your childhood: your bedroom, backyard, classroom, etc.

EXERCISE

Choose an unlined, spiral drawing tablet or a bound, blank- page book for your illustrated journal. Make sure the paper is of good quality so that you can use both sides, sketch in watercolor, or paste in photos. A cloth bound, blank book may inhibit you with its pristine beauty until you take pencil in hand and fill it up with writing and sketches that make it yours. If you want to make your journal and sketches part of your notebook, add loose-leaf sheets for the journal and another to hold your sketches.

Don't worry if your drawings aren't "good." They will be good for you because they will capture for you the essence of the thing you're thinking of in a way nothing else can.

When you're not working on a manuscript, write and sketch in your illustrated journal. Let it be a continuation of your thinking. Use simple language; the shortest distance between you and the publisher is clean, fresh prose. Study the masters: E.B. White, Beatrix Potter, Mark Twain. Use a good dictionary, a thesaurus, and a writing manual. Words and punctuation are tools that can work for or against you; know how to use them.

Don't worry that someone has already used your idea. If you write from the inside out, it will be your story.

PROGRESS CHECKLIST

- Get ready to begin by choosing a regular time and place to work.
- Make sure you have pencils and paper, a dictionary, thesaurus, and style guide at your work place.
- Do the exercises in this chapter (start your illustrated journal and do memory walk and reporter drawing.)

Reading List

These books provide a good role model library to start off with.

A Birthday for Frances *by Lillian and Russell Hoban*
Goodnight Moon *by Margaret Wise Brown*
The Little Bookroom *by Eleanor Farjeon*
Little Tim and the Brave Sea Captain *by Edward Ardizzone*
The House of Forty Fathers *by Meindert de Jong*
Charlotte's Web *by E. B. White*
The Court of the Stone Children *by Eleanor Cameron*
The Tombs of Atuan *by Ursula K. Le Guin*
The Tale of Peter Rabbit *by Beatrix Potter*
Harold and the Purple Crayon *by Crockett Johnson*
The Important Book *by Margaret Wise Brown*
The Runaway Bunny *by Margaret Wise Brown*
A Hole is to Dig *by Ruth Krauss*
Where the Wild Things Are *by Maurice Sendak*
Pat the Bunny *by Dorothy Kunhardt*
Noah's Ark *by Peter Spier*
Millions of Cats *by Wanda Gág*
Madeline *by Ludwig Bemelmans*
Curious George *by H. A. Rey*
Prayer for a Child *by Rachel Field*

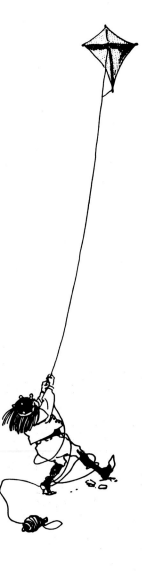

Chapter 3

WHAT IS IT?

FORMAT, THEME, AND AGE LEVEL

*E*arly in the process of writing your story, you will make important decisions about the length, tone, and theme of your book, as well as the need for illustrations and whether your characters will be animal or human. In the first flush of inspiration, your story may flow out in a form that feels "right," and you may not consciously weigh these choices as you make them. Later, you will want to consider the appropriateness of your decisions in the cool light of reason. You will find that the choices you make about format, message, and characters are motivated by one central factor — the age of your intended reader.

Like children, children's books come in many shapes and sizes. Even a subject like dinosaurs, which seems like a standard topic, may lend itself to different treatments appropriate for different formats and age groups. A book about baby dinosaurs and very small dinosaur species may be ideal for a very small-sized picture book, as well as for a small-sized reader who can relate to the special vulnerability these dinosaurs experienced on account of their diminutive size. If you want to emphasize the monumental scale of the most popular dinosaur species, you may want to visualize a very large book. In this case recognize that you will need to provide enough substance to justify your large-scale treatment.

Picture books depend as much on their illustrations as on their text. That's why, even if you're only going to write, it's important that you have an image in your mind of what the page is going to say. In picture books, the illustrations tell part of the story. Think of it this way: There's a

Case History (Berthe)

In 1961, I decided I wanted to illustrate children's books. We were living in Europe at the time and were coming home on a freighter to New Orleans for vacation. But I was pregnant with my fifth child and not allowed to travel by ship. I flew via New York, and on the advice of a writer friend, I brought with me a huge portfolio of drawings, the best of what I'd done in art school and some dreadful little stories I'd hastily written to go with illustrations to show an editor. Totally ignorant of the publishing world, I followed my friend's further advice. "Just barge right in," she said, "they're looking for talent."

I liked the books Harper & Row published, so I went there. Barging in hardly fits my timid, terrified entrance to Harper's office, but I have been lucky all of my life, and the person who literally opened the door at Harper was a kind, sympathetic young woman who took the time to look at my illustrations and stories. She liked the illustrations and she showed me how to make a book dummy. She told me I would then see how to pace my story and how to balance pictures and words. I know now that if she hadn't taken the trouble to encourage me, I wouldn't have pursued the idea of writing and illustrating children's books. And if I hadn't learned how to make a book dummy, I might never have succeeded in getting any story "right." Susan Hirshman, the young woman who opened the door at Harper's, is now one of the most respected editors in children's books; she is editor-in-chief of Greenwillow Books.

difference between an illustrated book and a picture book. Look at *The Tale of Peter Rabbit* by Beatrix Potter. You could read the text without looking at the pictures and you would not miss any of the story because the illustrations are not interpreting or adding to the plot. Beatrix Potter says nothing in the illustrations that she hasn't already said in the text. *Peter Rabbit* is an illustrated book.

Now look at *Where the Wild Things Are*. Maurice Sendak's pictures are indispensable to an understanding of the plot. In the beginning, Max, the little boy who misbehaves, is described as "making mischief of one kind or another." In the picture, you see that Max is nailing something into the wall and has been cruel to the dog. There are pages without any words at all where the monsters Max creates out of his fantasy grow bigger and more horrible. You can see the monsters dancing at the same time you see Max's expression showing that he's not afraid, he's brave and has it all under control. A lot of content is in the pictures, and writers who are not also illustrators must keep this in mind. *Where the Wild Things Are* is a picture book par excellence.

Remember that each page of your book will have a picture, and for your own sake, make a book dummy. A dummy of a picture book is a handmade book. It can include simple black-and-white line drawings or just verbal descriptions of what the pictures should show. Picture books are sometimes 24 pages long, but more often they contain 32 pages. All page counts in books are usually multiples of sixteen. Books are printed all on one big sheet of paper; eight pages are printed on one side of the sheet, eight pages on the other. The sheet is then folded and cut. These sixteen-page groupings, called signatures, are then gathered and bound to form the book. You need to know this information about page counts because you need to plan and present your book in a manner that is realistic from the manufacturing and marketing point of view.

You can always submit your manuscript by itself. However, your dummy can do double duty as a submission

tool. Publishers like to receive book dummies because they demonstrate that you are familiar with children's book formats. Your dummy can show that you are thinking visually. If your text is poetical or impressionistic, the dummy can convey important information about what you really want your book to communicate.

Imagining each page of your book will help you know exactly how much writing you have to do. It can also reassure you that your idea is big enough to make a picture book. Big is a relative term: Something big doesn't have to happen on every page.

Nothing big has to happen from page to page so long as everything that does happen helps communicate a clear, consistent theme. The *theme* is different from the *idea*

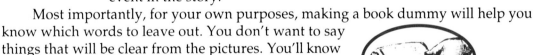

of your book. Your idea may be to write a book about baby dinosaurs. But your theme will be showing that, though they started out small, these dinosaurs grew big and strong and were soon able to fend for themselves. Think of the theme as the glue that holds your entire book together. Everything that happens must in some way illustrate this basic message, this universal element that children can relate to and take away with them as an opportunity for growth.

Don't let your book get didactic, though. Your theme should be illustrated by the events that happen in your book, not prosaically told in so many words. The theme should be below the surface of every event in the story.

Most importantly, for your own purposes, making a book dummy will help you know which words to leave out. You don't want to say things that will be clear from the pictures. You'll know how to pace your book and how to make the reader turn the page to find out what's next.

What publishers call children's books cover a very wide range of publishing. There are fancy hardbound books by famous writers with a few color plates thrown in (for instance, *Swan Lake*, by Mark Helprin and Chris Van Allsburg) that by no stretch of the imagination should really be called children's books. Such works are really adult books but get published and

marketed as children's books. These books have an art-book type of appeal, with beautiful design and production values.

On the other hand, there are very simple books of eight or twelve pages printed on cloth or vinyl. Such books are for the very youngest children and usually are so simple to plan and write that publishers rarely look to outside authors to execute them. This wide range of formats is one of the great opportunities before the children's writer. Because picture books may be convincingly presented in any of a variety of shapes and sizes, you can make a distinctive format part of your thinking for your book and part of your presentation to publishers.

Picture books can be softcover or hardcover; big or little; printed on cardboard or plastic; cut into shapes, or packaged with dolls. Be expansive in your thinking, but make sure the format you have in mind reflects the theme of your book. A perfect example is a project published long ago by Golden Books: a tall book about giants packaged with a tiny book about elves.

Be careful, however: Special format books are usually for quite young children. You must be sure that your subject matter, your ideal format, and your target reader all work together. A book shaped like a yellow school bus may sound like a fun idea; but do two-year-olds ride a yellow school bus? Format and age group are closely linked. Past age three or four, the standard 32-page picture book will be the norm. The publisher is usually the one to make exotic format choices. However, if you think a special feature or format would strengthen your proposal, go ahead and present your inventive idea to a publisher whose books demonstrate a level of comfort with innovative formats. After all, no one had published a "touch-and-feel" book before Dorothy Kunhardt came to Golden Books with the idea for *Pat the Bunny*. That book was the first of its kind and broke all sales records for children's books.

FORMATS BY AGE GROUP

Following is a rough grouping of children's book formats listed with the age groups for which they are designed:

6 months-2 years	cloth books; board books; floating bath books; "touch-and-feel" books; "shape" books
2 years-5 years	simple picture books; "toy" books with wheels, puzzle pieces, etc.; pop-ups and novelties
5 years-7 years	more sophisticated picture books; joke books; various kinds of informational books; simple easy-to-read books
7 years-9 years	more sophisticated informational books; chapter books
9 years-12 years	middle-grade novels and nonfiction
12 years and up	young adult (YA) novels and nonfiction

Planning is equally important if you want to write a chapter book or novel. You will know that this is the proper format if your story concerns children old enough to read for themselves. Chances are that you cannot write an entire novel in one burst of inspiration, as you sometimes can with a picture book. So instead of making a book dummy or writing out illustration suggestions, you need an outline spelling out chapter-by-chapter what will happen. You need not adhere slavishly to your outline once you get going;

CASE HISTORY (ERIC)

Sometimes a story does not stand strongly enough on its own to warrant publication without a special format treatment. At Golden Books we had a series of softcover picture books that were die-cut into different shapes. The goal was for each book's shape to resemble a big element in the story. Seymour Reit, a respected "easy-to-read" author, once submitted a charming poem about an old school bus that saved itself from the junk heap by flying. The story was appealing but nothing about it shouted "buy me." Then we remembered our shape-book series and decided to die-cut the book in the shape of a school bus. So The Flying School Bus was born! (See figure 24)

Using the book you are working on, change the characters from human to anthropomorphic or vice versa. Anthropomorphic characters are animal characters that display human traits, emotions and behavior. (See also Old Hannibal and the Hurricane, *figures 26 and 27)*

let the story move of its own force. A plan at the outset, a goal in sight with several smaller goals along the way, will keep your work in manageable segments so you can reach the great goal of completion.

New writers — and we have seen this often in our workshops — often err in creating elaborate fantasies for publication as picture books. Such stories often take the form of outer space adventures, or adventures underground or "through the looking glass." Think about the fantasies that have succeeded with young readers, the Alice books, the Oz series, *A Wrinkle in Time* — novels all. A rich, well-defined, meaningful fantasy world is almost impossible to create in the few words and few pages of a children's picture book. By the time you've explained your world and special characters, there's no more room to tell the story. Let yourself relax if your idea is to write such a story; expand your idea along clear, logical lines, and make sure you tell a cogent story. If you're thinking this way, try to cast your work as a novel.

Remember that small children tend to be literal-minded, partly because they don't have a wealth of associations for each new idea that comes along. Don't overwhelm picture book readers with too much to digest.

Visualize your characters and visualize a reader who is like them. Can they read? Can they write? Do they go to school? What grade? Is their focus home, or is it outside the home? Decide what kind of book you're writing by whom you see in your mind's eye.

Case History (Berthe)

There is something very comforting about an outline even if you don't intend to follow it exactly. First of all, it keeps your theme or goal firmly in your mind. You can think of the outline as a journey toward the goal, each chapter a step in that journey that brings you closer to the end. I was so nervous writing my first young adult novel, that I made an outline, or rather two woven together, because it was a time-warp story, part of it taking place in 1840 and the other in the present day. It comforted me to know when I was in one century, I knew where I'd emerge in the next. I worried about the transitions, but I actually enjoyed writing them because I had my outline to fall back on.

For the YA I am now writing, the sequel to Lost Magic, *I have divided a loose-leaf notebook into eleven segments, one for each of ten titled chapters and another for plans, ideas and outline. I do not write chronologically, that is, beginning at chapter one and ending at chapter ten. I think in bits and pieces and put those pieces into my notebook where they fit. This technique works for me and allows my characters the freedom to change the plot. Making an outline for your story and adapting it to your style of writing may mean that you crumple up your outline and throw it in the trash can, but it is worth a try!*

Exercise

1) *Think visually by writing illustration notes for your favorite fairy tales.*
2) *Retell your favorite fairy tale in your own words.*
   Break the text into thirty-two pages as follows:

       1/   *title page*
       2/   *copyright notice*
       3/   *half-title page*
       4/   *blank*
       5/   *Once upon a time. . . .*

   On a separate sheet of paper, write a one-paragraph description of the illustration you envision for each block of text. Be as detailed as you can, including ideas on perspective, cropping, color, etc.
3) *After completing your illustration notes, go back to your manuscript. Do you see places where you can cut words, where you need to change the pacing, where you need to say something different?*

Case History (Eric)

Make sure your format corresponds to your subject matter as well as to the age of your reader. Once Edith Kunhardt, daughter of the Pat the Bunny *author and author in her own right of* Pat the Cat *and* Pat the Puppy *and dozens of other books, developed a* Pat the Bunny-*type "touch and feel" book on the themes of God and prayer. I had to reject it despite its author's prominence, because in my opinion, novelty-type treatment of such a serious theme would seem to make light of it and turn off parents, as well as possibly sending a wrong message to children. By the same token, there are exceptions to every rule: Although books with animal characters are generally picture books for young children,* The Wind in the Willows *is a captivating novel that works for older readers.*

Case History (Eric)

I asked Isabelle Holland, the award-winning young adult novelist and adult mystery writer if she'd like to write a picture book on an inspirational theme. I knew Isabelle's wonderful writing and strong spiritual bent. She said yes, and turned in what was really a short story or novella about a cat following the procession of the three kings to Bethlehem. I'll never forget the overwhelming emotion I felt as I read the final manuscript in her presence when she came to deliver it. Moments like that make all editors' work seem worthwhile. The story and theme were so strong that they might have overwhelmed a picture book format. However, the fact that the protagonist was a cat helped us visualize the pictures, break the story into blocks of text, and publish this rather adult opus as The Christmas Cat.

Case History (Eric)

Sometimes your idea may be right for a storybook rather than a picture book. Phyllis Krasilovsky, award-winning author of The Cow Who Fell in the Canal, The First Tulips of Holland, *and many more, submitted a group of stories about a brother and sister. I first considered them for publication as individual picture books. But the individual stories — even the ones about birthday and Christmas — did not have the strength of the stories as a group, connected as they were by characters, themes, and a strong family feeling.*

Finally, I asked Phyllis to pen a foreword explaining the connections between the stories, and I published the lot as The Happy Times Storybook.

Self-Editing Checklist

Ask yourself these questions as you plan your book:
1. *When I visualize my book, what do I see?*
2. *How old are my characters? Are they animals? People?*
3. *How old are the readers who would be interested in my idea?*
4. *Are thirty-two pages too many? Too few?*
5. *Do I see a picture on every page?*
6. *Would a special feature — shape, a pop-up, etc. — add something to my idea?*
7. *If the book I visualize looks like another book, what book is that?*

Exercise

Read six of the books in the Reading List below and answer these questions:
1) *What is the theme of the book?*
2) *What age is the intended audience?*
3) *Would that story have worked in another format?*

Reading List

The books on this list have distinctive formats. As you look at each, try to discern the intended audience for each and note how the format adds something to the book.

What is Hanukkah? *by Harriet Ziefert*
Pat the Bunny *by Dorothy Kunhardt*
The Tall Book of Fairy Tales *illustrated by William Sharp*
The Little Fur Family *by Margaret Wise Brown*
The Nutshell Library *by Maurice Sendak*
Frog and Toad Are Friends *by Arnold Lobel*
Where's Spot? *by Eric Hill*

Chapter 4

WHERE, WHO, WHEN?

***

OR

SETTING, CHARACTERS, PLOT

*I*f we could give just one piece of advice, it would be to write about something you care about passionately. Don't be beguiled by what you perceive is a market trend. There may be an explosion of interest in dinosaurs, but if you, the writer, are sick to death of them or were never interested in them to begin with, it will show in your writing and your book will be just another lifeless manuscript sure to be rejected. A strong, personal interest in your subject makes it unique and gives it life.

You can prove this to yourself by writing a paragraph on a current, topical theme you are not terribly keen on. Now write a paragraph on something you care deeply about. Don't reread these paragraphs for at least one hour, preferably one day. When you come back to them you will see how much more vivid and thought provoking your second paragraph is than your first. You may even surprise yourself and find that your spontaneous writing done from the heart is far better than you believed you could do.

SETTING

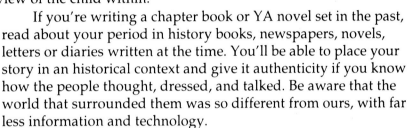

The same holds true for time and place. Set your book in a time that interests you, one that you've lived and know — or if it's in the past, one you'd enjoy researching. Even if yours is a picture book for very young children, make sure your setting is one you understand and feel comfortable in from the point of view of the child within.

If you're writing a chapter book or YA novel set in the past, read about your period in history books, newspapers, novels, letters or diaries written at the time. You'll be able to place your story in an historical context and give it authenticity if you know how the people thought, dressed, and talked. Be aware that the world that surrounded them was so different from ours, with far less information and technology.

Be sure your facts are correct. You will need to do a lot of research if your setting is historical, but if you like the period, research reading is fun, and it often presents you with new ideas to enrich your story. A sense of time and place is essential to your writing. If you, the writer, are comfortable and knowledgeable in a time and place, it will come

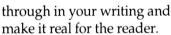

through in your writing and make it real for the reader.

For example, if your story takes place in the tropics, what kinds of flowers and plants might your characters encounter? What moods and colors bring to mind a warm sun, a blue sky, a soft breeze? What about the smell of jasmine? Suntan oil? A well-known author wrote about the "sweet scent of azaleas." Azaleas don't have a scent! Be careful. Don't make flowers bloom in the wrong season or

CASE HISTORY (BERTHE)

I have just completed a picture book, The Cajun Gingerbread Boy. *I began with a simple retelling of the folk tale and generic landscapes through which the gingerbread boy, a paper doll, runs (the pages are slit). My editor, Liz Gordon, who knows my background, suggested a Cajun retelling with Louisiana landscapes. I groaned and whined, something we strongly recommend against, but the book is now far stronger than my first draft because I know and love its setting. Even so, I spent the summer running around southwest Louisiana with my camera and sketchbook. I visited plantation houses, walked the fields of sugar cane, climbed fences and waded in bayous to bring home water hyacinths for painting. I enjoyed my research until I realized I was using it as an excuse not to face up to that clean, empty watercolor paper. But when I finally glued myself to the drawing board, I was comfortable in the Cajun setting I know and love.*

give them a fragrance they don't have.

If you are writing fantasy, you still have to abide by the laws your fantasy world dictates. There is no such thing in fantasy as a magic wand to make everything turn out all right just because the world of your book is imaginary. Fantasy requires research, too, best done by reading the classic fairy and folk tales, where you  will find there is more reality than fantasy and see that the fantasy must abide by laws sometimes even more rigid than those of reality! Begin with the works of George Macdonald, C.S. Lewis, and J.R.R. Tolkien.

If your book has a contemporary setting, your characters must act and think as today's children do. That's not as easy as it sounds. Each generation has a language, even a culture of its own, and whereas human nature doesn't change, customs and mores do. If you think you are au courant and Barney is in, he has been replaced by Power Rangers, who will no doubt be out by the time this book is printed. And even if you are a young writer, the manners and customs of a ten-year-old have changed since you were a child.

The best way to understand how children and young people behave and think is to observe them. Teachers, librarians and parents have a catbird seat, but even if you don't belong to one of those groups, you can still observe children at playgrounds and young people in their local hangouts. Movies give you a good idea of contemporary culture, and you can read books by authors popular with children who write about the way it is today, such as Judy Blume and Richard Peck, to name two of the best. Observation is all important, but don't forget what we've said about the child within and remembering how you felt as a child. Although that remains the same and almost universal, the way children act changes each decade if not seasonally, and although you don't have to like the changes, you have to be aware of them to speak to today's young people.

CHARACTERS

Concentrate on your characters. If you can make them believable to yourself, they will be real to your readers. "Real" characters will plot your book for you, almost as though they are telling you their story. This may sound like an exaggeration, but it's true and it works.

How can you create believable characters? The process is somewhat mysterious and varies with different writers. Characters often begin with a real person the writer has in mind and evolve into quite different people.

"Real" characters will never act "out of character." You cannot manipulate them to behave in a certain way if they would not do so in real life. If you have created a shy, introspective boy, he will not campaign for class president, much less get elected. However, if you have created an outgoing, unscrupulous boy, he might get himself elected by bending the rules. But perhaps his girl-friend, whom he hopes to impress, finds out about his secret deal and will have nothing more to do with him. And your shy guy? He's been in love with her all along and now when she looks around, there he is. Well, perhaps these are rather contrived characters and a thick plot, but they illustrate the important point that strong characters have a will of their own and can take over a plot.

When Louisa May Alcott wrote *Little Women*, her readers wanted Jo to marry Laurie, but Alcott knew that someone like her Jo could never marry a man like Laurie, and no matter how her readers begged, she refused to let it happen.

Dialogue is a powerful tool in characterization; it can also move your plot forward, show character development, and add to your story's credibility. Read some of the masters of dialogue in books on the reading lists (e.g., *Charlotte's Web* by E.B.

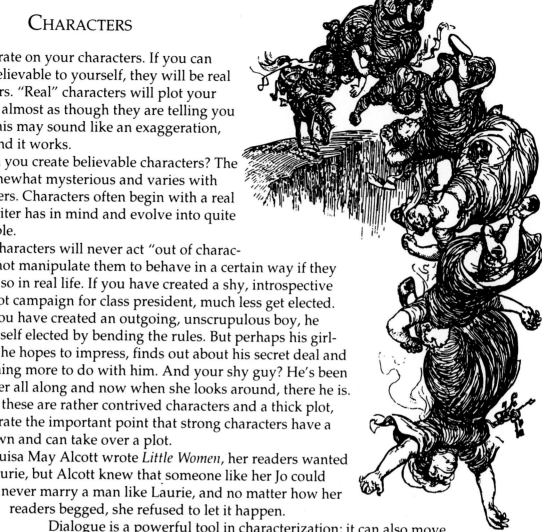

CASE HISTORY (BERTHE)

Lost Magic *is about Ceridwen, a fourteenth century "herb woman" who inherits magical power from a legendary sorcerer. But Ceridwen cannot use her gift until she develops it very much as a young person must study and hone her talents to achieve her full potential. Being an incurable romantic, I wanted Ceridwen to marry Robert, the handsome Lord of Bedevere, but given the times and Ceridwen's position in life, and in spite of her magical power, it could never have happened without weakening the whole story. Characters are real only when they behave as they would in real life.*

White) to see how they do it. Read your own dialogue to see if it is stilted or lacking character identification, and do the exercise at left.

PLOT

When you write your first draft, remember it is not set in cement. Just get it down on paper, and then you can fine-tune it, withholding information to create suspense, deleting parts that don't move your story along. You are very likely to get an idea when you are close to the end and you will have to change a large part of your story. If the change improves your story, make it.

A good editor will help you to say what you really mean but didn't know you knew. Careful polishing and self-editing will accomplish the same goal and possibly spell the difference between rejection and acceptance.

Put in its most simplistic form, a plot has a beginning, a middle, and an end. For the author, the beginning is usually the easiest, but difficulties may increase as you move toward a contrived ending. This progression is marked for the reader by increasing boredom and incredulity.

How many books have you read with great beginnings, bogged down middles, and incredible, manipulated endings? Here are some hints for avoiding these pitfalls:

If you don't have a great beginning, read through your manuscript until you hit something interesting. Start there and lop off the preliminary part, bringing in any omitted, necessary information later on. Hook the reader on the first page or you'll lose him to TV, soccer, or worst of all, to another author's better book.

A second important hint is to know where you're going, or rather, know where you can go if need be. Many's the promising beginning that was put aside because the author couldn't think of an ending. You don't have to stick to your preconceived ending, but it is comforting to have one. Make an outline or a plot summary, chapter by chapter. You don't have to stick to that either. In fact, your story will probably be better if you let your characters

change things. But having your outline and knowing you have a strong story line will comfort you and see you through even if your final story has a different ending.

The foggy, boggy middle: How to travel from a good idea to the perfect solution along an interesting path is not difficult if you've learned "the little red wagon" lesson (cf.

PLOT EXERCISES

Here are some exercises to get you thinking "plot."

1. *Take a classic fairy tale or a well-known folk tale and twist it in some way, writing for it a different ending, or changing the point of view of the storyteller.*
2. *Write an unwritten scene from a well-known Bible story. How did Jonah pass the time inside the belly of the great fish? Write this for the picture book age group. If you are an illustrator, draw the most powerful scene.*
3. *What if you were shipwrecked on a desert island? Write an account of your first day, noting how you feel and describing your surroundings in as much detail as possible.*

Case History), namely not to hang on to the first thought that crosses your mind. Play the "what if" game. Don't go down the obvious, trite, worn path in your mind. After you've done your first draft in a stream of consciousness style trying to get your ideas down, go over your writing looking for "little red wagons," clichés in words, situations, and characters.

Get your ideas down in writing, and then let your story sit in your mind overnight, over many nights if necessary. The "right" path, fresh and untrodden, will appear to you, and when you take it, you'll have thought through the middle of your story and taken your reader with you.

The middle of your book is your place to develop your characters further and increase the depth of your plot, always aware of the tension that is needed between the beginning and the ending of your story. Don't forget: You can always delete great chunks of unwanted writing if parts don't further your story.

CASE HISTORY (BERTHE)

A Tulane student of children's literature, Jennifer Rosen, wrote this delightful, twisted "Cinderella."

Once upon a time I was a lonely widow with two daughters to raise. Life was hard for us, but luckily I was introduced to a wonderful widower with a daughter of his own. We had a storybook romance and were soon married. He and his daughter moved into our home. From the beginning, it was easy to see that Cinderella was going to be a handful. She was used to having her father all to herself and wanted a lot of attention. To be honest, she was a brat. She was a beautiful child, but she was vain and selfish and spent most of her day looking in the mirror. My own children were going through a gawky stage at the time. They wore glasses and braces and Cinderella showed off her good looks at them and made them feel ugly and horrible.

When Cinderella's father died, my problems really began. I took on two jobs to support the three girls. Everyone in the house had to pitch in with the chores. The day of that famous Ball it was Cindi's turn to scrub the floors. She refused and threw a fit instead and stormed out the door in a huff. My dear Griselda finished her own work and then finished Cinderella's.

As soon as Griselda put away the mop, there was a puff of smoke and the fairy godmother appeared. Cinderella wasn't even home! The fairy godmother had come to reward Griselda for being so kind to her mother. I remember her words. She said, "When you're beautiful inside, you are also beautiful outside." She waved her magic wand and suddenly Griselda's glasses and braces were gone. She was transformed into a beautiful princess complete with gown, diamond tiara and glass slippers. Off she went to the Ball in her horse-drawn pumpkin carriage.

It was Griselda, not Cinderella that captured the heart of the prince that night! They danced until the stroke of midnight. Griselda was so happy she forgot the fairy godmother's warning to return home by 12:00. Suddenly her pumpkin coach disappeared and she found herself standing in her old clothes. Naturally, she ran home as fast as she could, leaving her slipper behind on the stairs. She ran over four miles, so you can imagine how swollen her feet were when she finally got home! Cinderella got home about the same time as Griselda. She had spent the night feeling sorry for herself. When Griselda told her about the wonderful time she had at the Ball, Cinderella was furious that she had missed it. You could just see her anger behind her smile.

The next morning, the prince and his palace guards came to the door to see who fit the glass slipper that was left behind at the Ball. Griselda's feet were still so swollen she couldn't fit them into the shoe. In a flash, Cinderella snatched the slipper and slid it on her own foot. (Both girls wore exactly the same size.) I tried to explain the true story to the prince, but he didn't believe in fairy godmothers and magic wands. The rest of the tale is history. Cinderella and the prince were married. They didn't exactly live happily ever after. I understand the poor prince is miserable because Cinderella is still the same selfish girl she always was. I call all the time to try to see her, but she never returns my calls.

Please set the record straight. Tell everyone that stepmothers want more than anything to be loved by their new family. Sometimes it's stepchildren who stand in the way of that happiness. Often the problem is communication. Everyone is afraid to express true feelings. But only by working together could they truly live "happily ever after."

WRITING EXERCISE FOR TIME AND PLACE

Think back to a vivid experience you've had, and write a paragraph not about the experience, but describing the setting. If it is inside, describe the interior using specific details: fine furniture, lighting, etc. If it is outside, what was the weather like? The plants and trees? What are some telling details (e.g., the music being played) that might give the reader a sense of time and place?

WRITING EXERCISE

YA: Write a one-page character sketch of each of your characters. This writing will not appear in your story but will help you get to know your characters.

PICTURE BOOK ILLUSTRATING EXERCISE

If you are an illustrator, draw or paint each character; if not, write art directions for the illustrations.

Case History (Eric)

You can make a reasoned decision about choosing anthropomorphic versus human characters. Joan Elizabeth Goodman submitted a story about a little girl named Rita and her first day of school. In the author's original sketches and manuscript, Rita would not go to school unless she could wear her bear costume, and her mother had to coax her from this idea. The bear costume signaled the author's unfulfilled urge to explore the "first day of school" theme using anthropomorphic characters. Anthropomorphic characters — or animal characters that exhibit human traits — can cross barriers of appearance, social class, etc., and therefore can be more universal than human characters. They may also help provide a welcome note of whimsy to make sensitive subject matter more palatable. Rita became a bear named Amanda, and her fears about school became warmer and more comfortable (see figures 21 and 22). Amanda went on to be an excellent vehicle for other emotional early-childhood topics such as coping with a new sibling.

© Joan Elizabeth Goodman

Case History (Berthe)

An elderly cousin once told me the story of how, as a young woman in the thirties, she'd been told by her Aunt Evaline and my grandmother to visit our family tomb to check on cleaning men who were preparing it for a burial. In those days in New Orleans, we had above-ground tombs; our family tomb was only large enough for one coffin, and burials had to take place nine months apart. Ivy told me that the problem was that Aunt Kate had died only six months after Uncle Ben, and so when the men were preparing the place for Aunt Kate, they found Uncle Ben very much intact, to make a ghastly pun. When Ivy arrived, she saw Uncle Ben in his coffin; a breeze passed over him and he disintegrated before her eyes, leaving a skeleton. She rushed home to our family to explain that Uncle Ben had not departed, another ghoulish pun, and why Aunt Kate would have to be buried elsewhere. Their eccentric reaction was that our family tomb was a kind of "second home" and under no circumstances could Katie go to a "strange new place." I wrote a short story about this event or rather the short story, "How We Moved From St. Louis #2," wrote itself. I showed it to Charlotte Zolotow at Harper, knowing it was not for children, but Charlotte liked the characters and suggested I put them into a YA novel. Secret Lives was the result. The cemetery incident is in the book but is not central to the plot. Aunt Evaline, Aunt Kate and others become characters different from their true selves, but their reactions to circumstances remained as they might have in real life.

Case History (Berthe)

After I'd written and illustrated several picture books, I fell in love with the written word and wanted to write a longer book. I wanted to write about the imaginary daughter of Marie Laveau, the Voo Doo queen, half-white and half-black, living in the wonderfully mixed culture of New Orleans in the 1840s. I was uncertain about writing a chapter book; I considered myself an illustrator, and even the short text of a picture book had not always come easily to me. But time and place fascinated me and I began reading firsthand accounts of life in New Orleans in the early and middle eighteenth century. I found collections of letters, reports, and two newspapers on microfilm at the Tulane library. Because my children were still small, I had little time. I did my writing in the wee hours of the morning and my research in the afternoon when they napped or played. The more I read, the more I wanted to read. I began to suspect that I'd missed a vocation — researcher. I felt very comfortable with my characters in the nineteenth century because now I knew what their world was like and what they thought about it.

Self-Editing Checklist

Check your story for plot situations and solutions which are trite because they are the most obvious, the thing you thought of first. Always be suspicious of quick solutions to forwarding your plot.

Case History (Berthe and Eric)

When we started writing this book, our editors who had seen the first chapters and an outline made the suggestion that we should expand the case histories (then only one short paragraph each) and send them an "annotated table of contents," a much more detailed outline of what we intended to do in each chapter.

These suggestions were very helpful to us in organizing our vast amount of material into a cohesive whole. An important thing to remember is that an editor looking at your book professionally can see its strengths and weaknesses better than you can, and give you direction.

EXERCISE

If you are writing a chapter book, make an annotated table of contents or plot summary for the book you are now writing. Divide the book into chapter headings, and under each heading, write a short summary of what happens in that chapter.

SELF-EDITING CHECKLIST

Place: Does your writing give you a sense of place? What details in your writing could be true only in the place about which you are writing?

Time: Does your writing "tell time?" What details could be true only in the time about which you are writing?

Characters: Ask the following questions about each of your characters:

1) *Is this character "faceless," or does he/she seem like a real person?*
2) *Does the character always act "in character?"*
3) *Do your characters' actions determine your plot, or does your plot bend your characters out of shape?*

Plot: Does your story move forward relentlessly, or does it go off in different directions?

Does your story have suspense and tension, or is your ending predictable?

Is your story didactic? Remember that although you want your reader to come away from your book enriched, you do not want to write a little sermon to get your lesson across.

READING LIST

Only Connect *by Sheila Egoff*
Telling Writing *by Ken McCrorie*
Books, Children and Men *by Paul Hazard*
Writing for Children and Young People *by Lyn Wynham*
Writing for Children *by Ellen Roberts*

Chapter 5

MAKING EVERY WORD COUNT

WRITING AND POLISHING

*I*t is said that writing cannot be taught, that writers are born, not made, but we believe that you can learn writing skills and that these will "free" you to write. Your own special creativity can be expressed only through and to the extent of your writing skills.

In this chapter, we will show you how to acquire writing skills and how to polish your writing until every word counts.

LEARNING ABOUT WHAT'S GONE BEFORE

In many schools today, "creative writing" is taught in early, elementary grades before grammar. By third grade, children have made their own books. The theory is that writing helps reading. The down side of this approach is that children must eventually learn grammar rules or their power to communicate their ideas in writing is diminished. As we have said before, it is essential to give a publisher a grammatically correct, neatly typed manuscript.

Rules must be learned so that you can break them, but you must learn them first. That is not as facetious as it sounds. Another way of putting it is: Grandchildren cannot come into the world before their parents and grandparents, and Maurice Sendak couldn't have written and illustrated *Where the Wild Things Are* before Wanda Gág blazed the picture book trail with *Millions of Cats*, the first true picture book in which the illustrations carry part of the story and are vital to an understanding and appreciation of the book as a whole.

It is important for you to know what has been done and what is being done in children's literature. If you have never had a survey course in children's literature, you should familiarize yourself now with what has been written for children in the past. At the end of this chapter, we have listed books to help guide your reading, and there are two extensive lists of current

titles compiled by a teacher and a reviewer at the end of the book. There is also a list of classic, trend-setting books of the eighteenth and nineteenth centuries to help you see the kinds of books children read in the past.

When you study children's literature, you will see that present-day books are built on the foundations of earlier books and that children's books reflect the times in which they were written. For example, you will notice that before World War II, many subjects were taboo in children's literature. Now there is scarcely a subject that has not been written about, from sex to drugs, although of course, controversial subject matter is handled with discretion. How you handle your subject matter will spell the difference between acceptance and rejection.

Notice, too, that in Victorian times, when children were meant to be seen and not heard,

their books were filled with decorous role models, showing children formally dressed, and speaking and acting in proper, often stilted, style. Young villains, if they appeared at all, were presented without sympathy.

After World War II, along came Maurice Sendak, who, in *Where the Wild Things Are*, presented to the youngest reader the interior, dark side of his very own, young self. Other writers joined him in "telling it like it is" in children's books. Compare Maurice Sendak's twentieth-century illustrations of little people with Kate Greenaway's nineteenth-century ones for a stunning contrast.

THE ANATOMY OF A BOOK

If we could just figure out exactly what makes a book a best-seller and a classic, we'd be able to create one ourselves. It may not be possible to identify all the ingredients that will give us foolproof success: Indeed, some classics defy all the rules, such as E.B. White's *Charlotte's Web*, as mentioned earlier. However, if you examine a classic, any book that has stayed in print for twenty-five years, you will find clues that help you in your own writing.

One of the most important clues is that every classic has the children's stamp of approval on it; it has been chosen by children who, as Paul Hazard said in his *Books, Children and Men*, refuse to be bored by books. It doesn't matter how much hype the publisher, educator or parent places on a book, a child will not read a book he doesn't like. But when children find one they love, they will claim it and hang on to it through generations — even if the

book was not written for them, such as Daniel Defoe's *Robinson Crusoe*, and even when those adults who "know best" proclaim it unworthy of literature, such as all of Dr. Seuss in the beginning, and most of Judy Blume still. Study classics of the past to find the qualities with child appeal that you can apply to your own work.

We asked a thirteen-year-old boy what he looked for when choosing a book, hoping to identify clues to child appeal. Without hesitation, he said, "Suspense, mystery, and action!" When questioned further, he added, "I like reality, books about now and the future."

Judging from the popularity of series books such as *Sweet Valley High* or *Goosebumps* we think this is a typical young adult response, although the part about reality may not be as universal as suspense, mystery, and action. This is not to say that fantasy, romance, history, and other genres are out. There are popular books that prove that a good book can come out of any genre and that classics often defy attempts at classification or anatomization.

To go back to what we said previously that the *skill* of writing good prose can be taught, we are saying that if you build into your story suspense, mystery, and action, you are building in appeal to your young audience. This is true not only of novels and chapter books but also of picture books. There has to be something that keeps the reader turning the pages. Don't forget that young people will read only the books they want to read.

CHARACTERS IN CHAPTER BOOKS AND YA NOVELS

Your characters must be well rounded and believable in order to make the reader care about what happens to them. If you feel that your characters have blank faces or interchangeable faces, try writing a character study for each. Do this for your eyes alone. Try to visualize and *write down* everything you can think of about your character's appearance, disposition, family and peer situation. Get to know this person as you might a friend or family member. What are the problems your character faces? If you are writing a young adult novel, chances are it will encompass coming-of-age obstacles. What are they? What unique characteristics does your character have that will influence

a response to these obstacles? Who are your character's peers and authority figures? Again going back to what we've said previously, your "real" characters will help you to plot your story. Real characters are the ones who will stay in the minds of readers and who can turn your book into a classic. Even if you are writing a picture book, your characters must still ring true.

SETTING

Once you have chosen your setting, be certain you know everything possible about it either through your own experience or meticulous research. Each setting has unique advantages and disadvantages. Make sure you understand them: One false move in a setting unfamiliar to you but lived in by your readers will destroy your credibility.

MYSTERY

If you are writing a mystery, the most important phases of your writing will be in the planning and polishing stages. In the planning stage, be sure you know how the mystery will be solved. Many is the promising mystery that has a disappointing ending because the writer did not figure out a believable, satisfying conclusion ahead of time.

In the polishing stage, especially if yours is a story that almost wrote itself and that

you were able to get down on paper quickly, read your story carefully, looking for places you can withhold information from your reader or mislead your reader (while at the same time maintaining the truth in the situation) into thinking in the wrong direction. You are aiming at an "Aha!" ending, one the reader must not suspect as he or she reads through the middle of the book.

SUSPENSE

Suspense is closely tied to mystery and tension. As your story progresses, the middle of your book is filled with obstacles, seemingly insurmountable, facing your protagonist. Again, be sure you, the writer, have figured out how those obstacles will be surmounted. Many times you will find that the solution is not readily visible to you. Don't give up. Let your plot problems simmer — for days, if necessary. The best, most exciting solutions are seldom the first you think of; they are usually the ones that occur to you suddenly, sometimes unexpectedly. That happens because your writing mind has been busy working on the problems while you were outwardly concerned with your daily life.

ACTION OR ADVENTURE

By now you will notice that mystery, suspense and action are so closely intertwined that they might all be included under the same umbrella and that ultimately that umbrella is characterization.

POLISHING

Go over your manuscript for mystery, suspense, and action looking for information you give your reader too soon and for "red herrings" (false trails) you might add.

Make every word count. Go over your writing and remove all unnecessary adjectives, adverbs, and trite expressions. Get in the habit of rejecting the first descriptive word that comes into your head. If you don't have to say it, don't; if you do, make your reader hear or see it.

We are, of course, assuming that you will check your manuscript for grammar, spelling, and typos. If you are shaky in these areas, use your computer's capabilities or ask a literate friend to copyedit for you. Never let a manuscript leave your hands unless it is the best you can do.

THE ANATOMY OF A PICTURE BOOK

There is no better way to learn than to scrutinize the work of published authors. Trying persistently to figure out how that other writer did it can be helpful, though it can sometimes diminish the joy of reading if you practice it constantly.

Here are a few from the many classics you can "dissect," looking for what makes them beloved:

Goodnight Moon (perhaps the most difficult to analyze)
Where the Wild Things Are
"Cinderella"
"Snow White"
"Beauty and the Beast"
Millions of Cats
Little Women
The Adventures of Tom Sawyer
The Tale of Peter Rabbit
Are You There God? It's Me, Margaret
The Cat in the Hat

In studying the anatomy of books, or what gives them child appeal, you will notice that the reader is drawn by identifying with a character or perceiving a familiar situation. There may be an obstacle one of the characters successfully surmounts. To paraphrase Bruno Bettelheim in his *The Uses of Enchantment*, there is, hidden in the tale, something which helps a child find meaning in life. Too lofty? Doesn't encompass books meant to amuse only? Yes, it does. Stretching the imagination, exposure to visual art, humor, are all necessary to cognitive growth.

In classics, you will notice that there is also a strong theme and a tension that keeps the reader turning pages. Try to identify the theme.

In traditional art schools, students learn the basics of drawing and painting by studying the Old Masters. They draw from life and from plaster busts, learning about composition, value, shape, and design, and they sit in museums and paint copies of masterpieces, trying to discover how the artist did it. This method of learning, applied to studying the classics, can help writers as they try to communicate their own ideas to readers through writing and illustrating.

Think of this applied learning technique as a course entitled The Anatomy of a Book. For example, let us consider *Millions of Cats*, by Wanda Gág. Wanda Gág knew and loved the classic fairy tales of the Brothers Grimm. She helped raise her orphaned sisters and brothers, and so she knew, too, what children liked. Her parents had been artists, and she became a printmaker in the twenties when that art form had a renaissance in this country and when publishers first opened departments solely devoted to children's books.

Millions of Cats is probably the first true American picture book in which the illustrations play as large a role as the text.

Here is an anatomical study of *Millions of Cats*:

1) The story begins like a folk or fairy tale with "once upon a time" and all the information the reader needs summarized on the first page.

2) There is no characterization. We know only that an old man and an old woman are childless and lonely.

3) Still on the first page, and in the first paragraph, we learn the entire situation: The old man will go on a journey to find a cat to cure their loneliness.

4) Again like the folk tale, the setting is any place and our time is any time. There is very little setting description.

5) The simplicity of the story line and the clean prose throughout — not an extra word anywhere — gives this picture book its classic quality. The page is carefully designed as an art form in itself: the text is in cursive writing, and the small house and the peasant-like couple are anybody and any place. The wide, white border forms a frame for the whole.

6) The design of the book flows after the first page. The little old man walks over hills rolling from page to page, punctuated by clouds similar to stepping stones. Now, we are accustomed to picture books in which the illustrations help carry the story, but this was a new concept in the twenties, originated by Gág.

7) Above all, notice how the illustrations do more than just illustrate the text, e.g., the reader can see the little cat grow from scrawniness to beauty.

8) Ask yourself why this book has remained in print since its publication in 1928, and you will see that the clues are in its anatomy; those are the aspects of a classic you can apply to your own work.

9) Although color is considered essential in most books for children, *Cats* is black and white. Printmaker that she was, Wanda Gág considered black the most beautiful of colors; she was at the press when her book was published, insisting that the black be truly black and not dark gray. (If you can find an early edition of *Cats* and compare it to the paperback one now in print, notice the difference in the quality of the black.)

Writing the Text of a Picture Book

If you are writing a picture book, it may help you to think of this genre as similar to poetry and your book as an illustrated prose poem. Obviously, your text must be short like a poem to accommodate a very young child's short attention span. Each word of a poem or picture book is important to express as clearly and as richly as possible your idea. That limitation forces you to choose words carefully and to eliminate ruthlessly words that are unnecessary. Again, like a poem, there should be only one simple idea, and every word must contribute to expressing that idea to make it comprehen-

Choose a classic (a book in print for more than twenty-five years). Do an anatomy of it.

Where does an illustration carry part of the story line not in the text?

Summarize the plot.

Look for clues which you believe have made this book a classic. In short, how did one illustrator/artist do it? Do an anatomy of your own book in dummy form, and correct what you perceive to be faults.

If you are writing a longer chapter book or a young adult novel for children, you can apply the same anatomy-of-a-book technique using your favorite book in that genre.

sible at a young child's level of experience. A four year old, for example, might not understand the evils of war, but he can be shown that it is cruel to kick a dog.

WRITING THE TEXT OF A CHAPTER BOOK

Because the text of a picture book, typed and double-spaced, is usually not much more than two pages long, it is obvious that every word counts; but if you are writing a book for older children, it is also true, although not as obvious. Read the first two pages of E.B. White's *Charlotte's Web*, then close the book, and in your own words, write that much of the story. When you reread White's version, you will be more aware of his clean, concise prose, the power and depth of his communication. Fern sees the situation from a child's point of view: It isn't fair to kill a pig just because he's the runt of a litter. Then you see the situation from her parents' point of view: Fern has to grow up, they are thinking, and learn that sometimes things in life are necessary even though they are not fair.

DIALOGUE AND LANGUAGE

Notice the dialogue on those two pages. The characters talk like real people, and the story is carried along and characterization developed within the quotation marks.

Nancy Willard's *The Sorceror's Apprentice* is another excellent book to study for an appreciation of the richness of language. Extravagantly designed and gorgeously illustrated by Leo and Diane Dillon, what child (or adult) would not fall in love at first sight with Sylire, the apprentice, and tremble with delectable fear at Willard's word picture:

"The house had fifty-seven doors
That snapped and growled
And groaned and roared,
And Knockers made of gnashing teeth,
Which mercifully hung out of reach."

But where are the adjectives? How does Willard give us such a vivid image? How does she tell the entire story always choosing the right word and never forcing a rhyme? Pore over this

book, enjoying and thinking about how it's done.

There are many old and modern classics to read and learn from, and the more you study, the more you'll understand what makes a classic and how you can turn your own ideas into good books for children.

MORE POLISHING

After you've written your story, perhaps in a stream of consciousness style, you may find it is just the way you want it to be. Double-check it for tense discrepancies, trite adjectives which are so overused they have lost their power (beautiful, awesome, great, happy), and stock phrases (quick as a wink, skinny as a rail). Look for wordy, boring explanations of things that can be shown in an illustration, left unsaid, or shown through dialogue, such as, "She had a winning smile" or "She sighed in resignation."

Every time you come across an adverb or an adjective, think about it. Does it convey anything? Could it be translated into a verb: "She ran fast" into "She raced"?

Complex sentences that confuse rather than clarify, run-on sentences, paragraphs that never end may seem unimportant in your grand plan of the whole book, but a reading editor does not have time to teach you basic writing skills and will usually reject a sloppily written manuscript, even if it has the possibilities of becoming a good book.

Take advantage of your readers' senses of taste, smell, sight, and feel. Don't tell your reader the landscape is beautiful; describe it so that the reader believes she is in that place. Don't tell your reader the hero of your book felt sad; instead, describe what has caused the hero's feelings.

In the theater, there is a tradition that a tragic actor must never cry; the actor must make the audience weep (e.g., Charlotte's death in *Charlotte's Web*).

PROGRESS OR SELF-EDITING CHECKLIST

Check your manuscript for:
1) *spelling and grammatical errors*
2) *unnecessary or meaningless words*
3) *tension*
4) *satisfying ending*
5) *Are you writing about something you care deeply about that comes from a child-like point of view?*
6) *Has it the power to expand a child's vision and understanding of the world?*
7) *Does it involve the young reader's participation, either verbal, mental, or physical?*
8) *Will it enhance the child's cognitive or creative abilities?*
9) *Will it appeal to a child, attract and hold his attention, or have you allowed yourself to be carried away by something you want a child to know?*

READING LIST

Telling Writing *by Ken Macrorie*
The Uses of Enchantment *by Bruno Bettelheim*
Only Connect *by Sheila Egoff*
Children's Books in England *by Harvey Darton*
The Classic Fairy Tales *by Iona and Peter Opie*
Writing With Pictures *by Uri Shulevitz*
The Annotated Mother Goose *by William Baring-Gould*
Three Centuries of Books in Europe *by Bettina Hurlimann*
Children and Literature *by John Warren Steurg*
The Arbuthnot Anthology of Children's Literature *by May Hill Arbuthnot*
Books, Children and Men *by Paul Hazard*
Writing for Children and Teenagers *by Lee Wyndham*

CLASSICS OF THE SEVENTEENTH THROUGH NINETEENTH CENTURIES
Perrault's Fairy Tales *1697*
Robinson Crusoe *by Daniel Defoe 1719*
Gulliver's Travels *by Jonathan Swift 1726*
A Little Pretty Pocket-Book *by John Newbery 1744*
A Visit from St. Nicholas *by Clement Moore 1822*
Grimm's Popular Stories in English *(trans. Edgar Taylor)* 1823
A Christmas Carol *by Charles Dickens 1843*
Fairy Tales *by Hans Christian Andersen 1846*
Alice's Adventures in Wonderland *by Lewis Carroll 1865*
Little Women *by Louisa M. Alcott 1868*
The Adventures of Tom Sawyer *by Mark Twain 1876*
Treasure Island *by Robert Louis Stevenson 1883*
Robin Hood *by Howard Pyle 1883*
Heidi *by Johanna Spyri 1884*
The Adventures of Huckleberry Finn *by Mark Twain 1884*
The Jungle Book *by Rudyard Kipling 1894*

TREND-SETTING BOOKS OF THE TWENTIETH CENTURY
The Tale of Peter Rabbit *by Beatrix Potter 1901*
Millions of Cats *by Wanda Gág 1928*
Where the Wild Things Are *by Maurice Sendak 1963*

Chapter 6

ILLUSTRATION

he turn of the century — which produced such great illustrators as Howard
Pyle, N.C. Wyeth, and Arthur Rackham — is often called "The Golden Age
of Illustration," but if any period of time challenges the title, it is ours.
Children's books today are of unsurpassed quality and diversity.

Lucky the children who are exposed to the best of today's books! The first illustrations they see will whet their appetites and help to form their tastes for all forms of art,
even inaccessible museum and gallery paintings.

Because young tastes can be formed from the pictures children see in their first
books, it is our job as adults to give children as much informed variety as possible. Even
if you are not an illustrator, you need to have a good understanding of what's been
done, and what can be done, with illustration, and so in this chapter, we will address
both illustrators and writers of children's picture books.

There is more to book illustration than producing a pretty picture. An illustration
must relate to the text and illuminate it in some way; it must communicate something,
an emotion or an idea. An illustration in an illustrated book, intended for older children
or adults, usually expresses in graphic form a part of the text that has already been
expressed in words.

An illustration in a
picture book for very
young children goes a
step further and will
often carry part of the
plot. In some cases, the
illustrations carry the
entire plot, as in a wordless book, e.g., *Tuesday* by
David Wiesner.

Although illustra-
tions in picture books are

as important as the text, it doesn't mean that if you're a writer for very young children, you should be an illustrator, too, or even find one before submitting your picture book to a publisher. It does mean, however, that if you're going to write a picture book for very young children, you should have much more than a nodding acquaintance with illustration.

You might want to study the history of illustration from early eighteenth century wood block prints to the marvelous variety of today's illustrations. At the end of this chapter is a list of "milestone" books to guide you, as well as a list of books about illustration. But, as we've said before, the best way to acquaint yourself with what's been done and is being done is to visit your library and local bookstores, and to ask people involved in children's books (not forgetting the children themselves!) to tell you what appeals to them and why.

Good editors, art directors, and marketing people usually ask for changes from the writer and illustrator. They can see a book from the point of view of outside experts, and the changes they want are almost always "right." Just as often, they are almost always difficult for the creator to accept. A knowledge of children's literature will give you, as creator, a wide perspective and help you to see your work from an outsider's view as well as accept changes publishers may ask for. The bottom line is that everyone involved in a book for children wants that book to be successful, and each has a specialized expertise necessary for success.

The next thing you should do if you have not already done so is make a book dummy with sketches, even if you don't intend to show it to anyone. The process of

choosing what you want illustrated in your story and then deciding how it would be shown in picture form will increase your understanding of picture books as nothing else can. Later in this chapter — and previously in chapter three — we show you in detail how to make a book dummy. By making a dummy, you will learn more about the picture book genre than you can in any other way, and you will never look at a book for young

children again in the same way. You will understand the pacing in stories; notice unnecessary words; see where the illustration should carry the story instead of the text. You will understand the importance of page design and type-face, as well as the need and the ways to communicate your idea visually and verbally. You will become more aware of the aesthetics involved. Most important of all, you will see the picture book as a whole, an art form, a prose poem, and appreciate its potential for beauty and influence on young minds.

If you cannot (or will not) illustrate, you might have a friend or a child illustrate for your book dummy, or you can use photos, cutouts, hand-painted shapes and collages. You will be surprised at how beautiful a collage-illustration can be constructed from just torn pages from a magazine. If worst comes to worst and you are convinced you can't draw a straight line, then, as we've said before, do word pictures with descriptions of the illustrations you want for each page.

The following sections are designed to take you beyond personal taste and help you acquire an understanding of aesthetic values and creative tools — in short, to make you "visually literate."

Dr. Patsy H. Perritt, Professor, School of Library and Information Science, Louisiana State University, has contributed the following sections on Visual Literacy, Picture Book Format, Mediums and Art Notes in Books.

VISUAL LITERACY THROUGH PICTURE BOOKS

Just hearing words and finally learning to read and "feel words" adds immeasurably to one's life. The same is true for the visual world around us. The development of artistic awareness adds depth and richness to our experiences, whether those experiences are in the everyday world of work and play, in an art gallery or museum, or in a book.

In today's world of constant television, video games, and the barrage of advertisements delivered in a multitude of formats, children have a wide variety of visual experiences, yet they are often unaware of the visual clues to developing artistic awareness coming their way.

Children can be guided in the process of learning to read; they can also be guided in the recognition, understanding and appreciation of visual images. What better way to develop "visual literacy" than in the books they might already love or the books they might easily obtain in their schools and libraries?

This section will cover book design and mediums for

preparing art, as well as some descriptions of the picture book format that might be helpful in the preparation of illustration as well as useful to those seeking to guide children in "visual literacy."

As an author, it is important to know that you are not responsible for providing an illustrated manuscript. The publisher will employ an illustrator, and as strange as it might seem, most often the author and the illustrator do not collaborate. This will depend upon the personal practices of the editor and the general editorial policies of the publisher. The publisher also employs an art director, who usually works with the illustrator from earliest stages of creation to the final printing. The art director guides such decisions as size of the book; weight, color, and texture of the paper; typography; cover art and flap copy; placement of words and text; frontispiece and tailpiece material and illustration, as well as endpapers. Illustrators might have suggestions for one or more aspects of the design of a book, but they should know that art directors have special training and experience that will be invaluable in the process of producing a book.

If you are an artist and you wish to illustrate books for children, here are some basics of children's picture book illustration and book design that will help you to get started in the field. The close relationship of text to illustration in picture books makes unique demands upon the illustrator.

THE PICTURE BOOK FORMAT

LENGTH:

The standard length of a picture book is thirty-two pages in total. That means the illustrator has the back and front of sixteen pages to use, and those pages will include the half-title page, title pages (usually a double page), and another page for publisher's information and CIP (Cataloging-in-Publication) data. It is possible to utilize the endpapers, which are the back of the hard cover, referred to as "boards," and the page next to it in the front of the book and in the back of the book, but only for visual "suggestion," not for text. Decorative end papers are expensive and are not used on all books, but even the color and texture of end papers can enhance the mood of the story. The length of a picture book is usually thirty-two pages, or two signatures of sixteen pages each.

SIZE:

Consider the average size of a bookshelf, approximately ten inches deep and twelve inches high. Most publishers encourage a book size that will easily fit on a library shelf with the spine facing out and discourage wide diversion, such as long, skinny shapes that would stick out from a shelf, very small sizes that would easily get lost behind other books; or tall books that would have to be placed on a shelf by turning the book on its side. As you create illustrations, you will most likely have in mind the size and shape you think is most appropriate. You will need to consider the feeling that you wish to create within the viewer. Do the words need visuals that reinforce a sense of vastness, or coziness, or towering heights? Take a careful look at a variety of sizes and shapes, and ask yourself "Why is this size or shape important/ appropriate to the telling of the story? (See Wanda Gág's *Millions of Cats*, Don and Audrey Woods's *The Napping House*, and any of the Beatrix Potter tales in their original, small-book size.)

PLACEMENT OF WORDS AND ILLUSTRATIONS:

The illustrations need to be in close proximity to the words being illustrated. The illustrations can incorporate the text (an excellent example is Denise Fleming's *In the Small Small Pond*) or the text can be separated from the illustrations by design, such as placement in blocked space within the illustration or within borders that separate the text and the picture or on a facing page. There is no "right" way to place the illustrations, such as above or below the words. The illustrator must decide what is suitable placement for the mood and flow of the visual presentation. This also applies to the visual units on a single page or a double-page spread. A child who is learning to "read" visuals in a book needs a straight- forward, one-scene presentation, such as Nancy Tafuri's *Have You Seen My Ducklings?* or Lois Ehler's *Feathers for Lunch*. In planning the page layout and in executing the artwork, always consider the technical reality of the "gutter," the portion of the paper taken up by the binding. Allow at least one-quarter inch on the inner edge of each page for stitching, and design any double-page spread to accommodate the visual impact of the gutter. Never have the focal point of a two-page spread in the exact center of the double page or it will be "swallowed" in the gutter when the pages are bound. The illustration should be so composed that the viewer's eye will not be stopped by the strong vertical line created by the gutter.

STYLE AND SIZE OF TYPE:

An art director will provide guidance in the selection of typeface, size, and color, but you can offer suggestions as to why a particular style, size, and color seem to be in harmony with the story being told. Numerous samples can be found by inquiring at a local printing company, consulting books on typography and graphic design, or even by experimenting with the various fonts and sizes on personal computers. Legibility is always the key factor, but there is a range of possibilities in style, size, and color of the print.

BOOK JACKET AND COVER:
 Some picture books have separate paper covers or illustrated hard covers that could require additional illustrations. The first illustration seen by a potential reader must have persuasive powers. It must raise questions as to what might be happening within the book, thereby drawing the reader to open the book. The illustrator should consider the interest that could be initiated on the cover, proceeding across the endpapers to the half-title page and on to the title pages, possibly including the page for publishing and cataloging information.

MEDIUMS

 Today's books for children display a wide range of artistic expression. Today's reproduction technology allows the use of almost any medium and technique in the artistic expression of the message. Everything from quilts to relief sculptures can be photographed, the colors separated by laser scanner, and then painted. The following examples will indicate the infinite range of media being used, often in combination within a single illustration, to create a spectrum of visual effects:

WATERCOLORS —
 Dawn, illustrated by Uri Shulevitz; *Tuesday*, illustrated by David Wiesner

OILS —
 Hansel and Gretel, illustrated by Paul O. Zelinksy; *The True Story of the Three Little Pigs*, illustrated by Jon Scieszka

ACRYLICS —
 Working Cotton, illustrated by Carole Byrd; *Miss Rumphius*, illustrated by Barbara Cooney

INK —
 Millions of Cats, illustrated by Wanda Gág; *Mufaro's Beautiful Daughters*, illustrated by John Steptoe

PENCIL —
 Jumanji, illustrated by Chris Van Allsburg; *The Story of Jumping Mouse*, illustrated by John Steptoe

PLASTICINE —
 Two by Two and *Have You Seen Birds?*, illustrated by Barbara Reid Wood; *A Story, a Story*, illustrated by Gail Haley; *Drummer Hoff*, illustrated by Ed Emberley

METAL —
   Aida, illustrated by Leo and Diane Dillon (metal frame created by Lee Dillon)

TISSUE PAPER —
   Eric Carle's Animals Animals, illustrated by Eric Carle

CUT PAPER —
   Rain Player, illustrated by David Wisniewski; *The Paper Crane*, illustrated by Molly Bang

PAPER PULP —
   In the Small Small Pond and *In the Tall Tall Grass*, illustrated by Denise Fleming

FABRIC —
   Tar Beach, illustrated by Faith Ringgold (see borders); *Come to My Party* and *The Way Home*, illustrated by Salley Mavor

The techniques, or methods of creating the art, are equally varied, including painting, etching, wood and linoleum cutting, airbrush, collage, and photography:

AIRBRUSH —
   Freight Train, illustrated by Donald Crews; *Why Mosquitoes Buzz in People's Ears*, illustrated by Leo and Diane Dillon

COLLAGE —
   Window, by Jeannie Baker; *The Snowy Day*, by Ezra Jack Keats; *Red Leaf, Yellow Leaf*, illustrated by Lois Ehlert

PHOTOGRAPHY—
   Spots, Feathers, and Curly Tails, illustrated by Tana Hoban; *Bridges*, illustrated by Ken Robbins

ART NOTES IN BOOKS

As an illustrator, you can help in the process of educating our children about the art in your books by asking the publisher to include information on your mediums and techniques. This can be printed on the verso of the title page with the publishing and cataloging information or in the back of the book in the form of notes. Usually this is a brief notation, but in some cases the illustrator has given extensive description of the process and the materials, such as Yoshi's comments in *Who's Hiding Here?*

The following section is written and illustrated by Auseklis Ozols, head of the New Orleans Academy of Fine Arts. It is based on his course, Color and Design, in which he teaches students principles of art as applicable to illustration as they are to fine art.

BASIC CONSIDERATIONS OF DESIGN:

THE PLASTIC VALUES

The *plastic values* are the aesthetic tools of the artist. They are not subject matter or narrative content, but are the means by which they are expressed and the criteria for critiquing art and becoming visually literate. They are line, color, value, texture, pattern, and form.

1) LINE

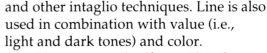

Line is the demarcation of separate planes, or the intersection of two or more forms. In reality, line does not actually exist, but the artist uses a pencil or pen line to indicate the beginning and end of particular shapes.

The overlapping of two different values creates an *implied line** (figures 1 and 2). *Drawn line* expresses the temperament and character of individual artists. *Line quality* is a condition that is imparted to the drawn line that renders it unique in expression.

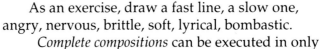

As an exercise, draw a fast line, a slow one, angry, nervous, brittle, soft, lyrical, bombastic. *Complete compositions* can be executed in only line, as in pencil and pen-and-ink drawings, etchings, engravings, and other intaglio techniques. Line is also used in combination with value (i.e., light and dark tones) and color.

Linear perspective (figure 3) is the two-dimensional representation of the third dimension. It is the study of the natural phenomenon where objects decrease in size as they recede farther back in space. The laws governing perspective require greater space than allowed here (suggested reading: *Perspective for Artists* by Rex Vicat Cole, Dover [22487-2].)

**Implied line is illustrated in figures 1, 2, 3, 4, and 5.*

2) COLOR

All color is contained in white light, which is a small part of the electromagnetic spectrum. By the use of a prism, white light is separated into its components, or the visible spectrum. The visible spectrum is like the rainbow: It starts with red, orange, yellow, green, blue, and violet, and it includes all transition colors. The color wheel was devised by bending the spectrum around until the red and violet connect.

Color may be the most expressive element of the plastic values. The moods and emotions that can be expressed by color are legion, cf section. The Terminology of Color, and the color wheel (figure 9).

3) VALUE

An important corollary of color, *value* refers to the relation of a color to black-and-white and all the grays in between. In order to change the value of a color, we must mix it with something lighter or darker than itself. By mixing white or black with a color, we change its value without changing its *hue*, which we indicate by saying *light blue* or *dark blue*. The knowledge of a scale of grays from white to black is indispensable to the artist (figure 4).

Color Perspective – Air, as well as water, is a substance composed of molecules, and it takes on specific color dependent upon the light quality of the day or time of day. On a cloudless, sunny day, the air color is blue, which reflects on everything it contains. On overcast days, the air color can be a variety of grays, during a sunset it can be orange, and so on. *Color perspective* is the expression of distance and space by the addition of air color to pictorial elements. The more air color is added, the further in distance objects appear.* The combination of linear and color perspective enhance greatly the sense of space (figure 5).

In the illustration shown in figure 6, page 66, red and green are used as subject colors, and a warm gray is the air color. The subject colors are reduced in intensity by the air color as they recede into the distance.

4) TEXTURE

Texture is a visual as well as tactile sensation. It is surface quality attributed to certain objects. Sand has its texture, the bark of a tree another, an angora sweater, the skin of a fish, etc.

We can express differences in texture by use of variance in line quality and different techniques of pigment application. Textural changes in a work of art add richness and interest.

5) PATTERN

Pattern is a repetition of a shape or combination of shapes. Any single shape, no matter how insignificant in appearance, when repeated in a regular manner, will create a lovely pattern. Pattern greatly enriches the visual dynamics of design. Pattern could also be described as *enlarged texture*.

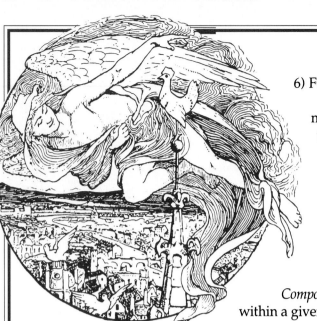

6) FORM

Form is a loose term applied to the perception of mass or volume, or the idea of solid objects in the third dimension. Yet air and water also contain form in the shapes of clouds and reflections. The sense of form is usually the desired result when the four previous values (line, color, texture, and pattern) are used in combination.

COMPOSITION

Composition is the conscious arrangement of the plastic values within a given space, as a canvas or paper, etc. *Design* is another term for the same. The greatest aesthetic strength of a work is usually attributed to the composition. If line, color, texture, pattern, and form are the divisions, then composition is the general in the army of aesthetics. *Composition* is the study of space division. It is the planning of intervals between occurrences. It is the setting of the stage for the optimum expression of the narrative.

DYNAMIC VS. STATIC

The word *dynamic* refers to the situation where motion is implied in a composition, and constantly holds the interest of the viewer. A static composition may be interesting enough, yet it does not incur the same excitement upon second and third viewing.

SYMMETRY VS. ASYMMETRY

Symmetrical compositions are usually static, yet can have a formal elegance. Asymmetrical compositions of the same subject usually hold more interest and allow the artist greater creativity in the organization of pictorial elements (figure 7).

SCALE

The sense of scale suggests proportional relationships between objects. Rocks, clouds, sand dunes, and waves are *fractiles*, shapes in nature that need human attributes to give them scale. Figure 8 illustrates this point by showing a similar rock in each sketch, in combination with two differing human attributes; in turn, each sketch presents the viewer with a completely different sense of scale.

The Terminology of Color

THE PRIMARY COLORS — red, yellow, blue (figure 9 — double line triangle)

    In pigment mixtures, these colors are called *primary* because they cannot be obtained by mixtures of other colors. All other colors are obtained by mixtures of the primaries.

THE SECONDARY COLORS — orange, green, violet (figure 9 — single line triangle) are obtained by mixtures of adjacent primaries.

THE TERTIARY COLORS — yellow orange, yellow green, blue green, blue violet, red violet, red orange are obtained by mixtures of adjacent primaries and secondaries.

COMPLIMENTARY COLORS — colors that are opposite on the color wheel (figure 9 — connected by straight dotted lines); complimentary colors when placed next to each other produce strongest contrast.

TINT, TONE AND SHADE —
    A *tint* is a mixture of pure color with white.
    A *tone* is a mixture of pure color with gray or its complement.
    A *shade* is a mixture of pure color with black.

HUE is the term used for the family of color as found on the color wheel.

CHROMA is the strength or brightness of a hue. Example: Pthalo green has greater chroma than earth green.

It is interesting and helpful to note how very differently illustrators work. There is no correct way to illustrate, and your way can draw its strength from being unique. The following three case histories for this chapter are more detailed and expanded than those in the rest of the book. They are, as much as possible, demonstrations of actual book projects. These case histories are written by Jean Cassels, illustrator of numerous nonfiction picture books; illustrator Emily McCully, Caldecott medalist in 1992; and Berthe Amoss, illustrator of picture books and author of this book.

Case History: Jean Cassels and *Prairie Dogs* (Scholastic)

All assignments begin with a call from my agent. She discusses with me the company, designs, schedule, and budget. Once we've agreed, she will send me a job order and contract.

Depending on the nature of the assignment, storybook, textbook, or part of a larger reading program, the instructions from the art director will be more or less specific. On this project, Prairie Dogs, I was given nearly 100 per cent artistic control. I received page layouts with the manuscript in place, but I was able to rearrange it as needed to best design the page with my art.

To begin, I read the manuscript, looked at the page layouts, and then did thumbnail sketches of each page for the entire book. This overview of the book helps to get a good balance of light, dark, colorful, quiet, up-close view, far-away view, action, calm, left-to-right movement, right-to-left movement, heavy on top, or heavy on the bottom.

When doing the actual sketches, I kept a notebook to record my references for each page. Next to the manuscript page number, I wrote what the reference was for — plants in background or paws of prairie dog — then I recorded the reference information — book title and page or scrap or personal photo. This saved me time and frustration when going back to do the finishes. I recommend maintaining a clip file, collecting books, and taking lots of photos.

For Prairie Dogs, I spent many hours at the Audubon Zoo observing, sketching, and taking photos of prairie dogs. This was an invaluable experience, helping me to understand their posture, movements, and interactions.

After completing the sketches, I made copies of each one. The sketches went to the designer at Scholastic with their page layouts.

When the sketches are returned, I'm always hoping to see: Good! Great! But sometimes there will be comments, or suggestions or requests for changes — sometimes small, sometimes large — even needing new sketches. At this point, you can discuss with the client and their consultant why you did what you did, using the reference that you had. If you've done your research well and explain your sketch and ideas well, perhaps they will let it stand. Otherwise you will have to make the changes. The point to remember in all of this is not egos but to make the best book possible.

My sketches are done in pencil on graphics 360, 100 per cent rag translucent marker paper. The finished work is done on 140-lb. hot-press Arches watercolor paper in gouache. Before beginning the finishes, I check my sketches against the reference and tighten up the sketches, making any changes I feel are necessary or to follow their comments for changes (figure 10).

I attach the sketch to the back of the watercolor paper, and working on a light box, I outline carefully the drawing, still working from my reference as well as the sketch.

I check my thumbnail sketch for colors and do a larger color sketch; then I mix my colors to begin the painting.

I lay in large washes, and working carefully, I go from the general to the specific (figure 11). On this book, Prairie Dogs, the very last thing to do was prairie-dog whiskers!

Before sending the finishes off to the client, I check each painting for any last touch-ups (figure 12). I clean up any smudges or fingerprints on the margins and erase all unnecessary pencil lines. I have to be certain that the corrected page number is written on each painting, along with the job number, job name, my name, and my agent's name.

Parchment is attached to each painting to protect it, and all the paintings are put together between heavy cardboard, with a cover letter to the designer stating what I'm sending and which book it is for.

Case History: Notes on Work, Emily Arnold McCully

As I always remind school audiences, I am an illustrator, not an artist. Every picture is composed to serve a text, or narrative, and therefore I know in my head at the outset how I want it to turn out (whether or not I succeed). An "artist," in my view, is an explorer who embarks without an end in mind.

Given this clear goal, I still try foremost for a look of liveliness and spontaneity in the work (figures 13, 14, 15, and 16). Readers must be able to enter into pictures for them to work as narrative elements. A gorgeous surface can be forbidding. I keep my sketches loose until the very last minute, submitting dummies that require a lot of imagination to interpret. I never use color until the finish stage, so that there remain a great many problems to solve. I hope that the energy it takes to solve them will invigorate the painting.

I am most interested in characterization and action — characters doing things that help to reveal them and give the pictures dramatic power. It's like making up a movie. I seldom use models, so the effort is to translate what's in my head to the page. This is always more or less agony. Often, I will redo a picture many times just to get a small face right. Very seldom does the paint perform some unexpected miracle on its own. This did happen in a recent book set in Ireland, where watercolor naturally helped create misty seascapes, to my delight.

I am setting books more often in the past. I research costumes and settings in library books and the Picture Collection, a quaint enclave in the NY Public Library, which houses thousands of clipped photographs from various sources. I am very impatient with this sort of thing, since my penchant is for the scrawled line drawing. But having to pay attention to details and get them right has improved my work. I have noticed that many artists seem to "do things the hard way," working against their natural instincts or even abilities, and I am certainly one of them.

Every story is different and calls for different sorts of illustrations. Over the years, my style has never been fixed, because of this, I don't usually plan on a palette, but it seems to emerge differently every time, even though I rely mostly on a limited set of dry watercolors of the sort children use. This has been supplemented lately by tubes and pastels. I purchased the latter singly and without anything in mind, so their range is also an accidental determinant. It used to be that color and depth were lost in printing, but technology has improved. Still, original art still looks much more alive than the books.

© Emily Arnold McCully

CASE HISTORY: BERTHE AMOSS AND *THE CAJUN GINGERBREAD BOY* (HYPERION)

I read and loved the classic nursery tales and fairy tales as a child, but I fell in love with them when I taught children's literature. The stories provide so many levels of satisfaction and evoke visual images, which beg to be illustrated. And, of course, the classic tales are in the public domain, fair game for any writer or illustrator to interpret or twist.

I chose "The Gingerbread Boy" because I remembered loving the refrain "Run, Run, fast as you can! You can't catch me, I'm the Gingerbread Man!" I also remembered being upset over the ending, "And that was the end of the gingerbread man." I wanted to change the ending without damaging the integrity of the tale. I also wanted to do a book that was half toy and could be played with as well as read.

I made a book dummy to show my editor with a separate, paper doll Gingerbread Boy traveling through slit pages of Louisiana landscapes. I secured the paper doll to the cover with a cookie cutter and wrote a recipe on the back to resurrect him.

The Cajun Gingerbread Boy was born, and growing with it, as in all picture books, were its own, unique set of problems and solutions involving many people and changes.

My editor, Elizabeth Gordon, eliminated the cookie cutter as superfluous (thank goodness — what a packaging nightmare that would have been!) and asked me to "cajunize" the text. The wolf in the story immediately turned into an alligator, and the text was adapted with the help of Cajun cousins and Coleen Salley, professor of Children's Literature at the University of New Orleans and a master Cajun storyteller.

The cover presented the biggest problem. We had to secure the paper doll and get the slit-page concept across to the reader while the book was still shrink-wrapped.

In the cajunizing process, I had gone to great pains to make the alligator look realistic, studying alligators at the zoo, in the bayous, and, of course, in National Geographic *magazine.*

I hand-printed the title in letters made to look like gingerbread (figure 17), but before the cover got to the printer, Ellen Friedman, the art director, changed my letters to far more legible ones in red.

The slit jaws holding the gingerbread boy worked fine until the book went into production. At that point, in order to make the gingerbread boy fit into the jaws, the printer had to duplicate the alligator and paste him on top of the original one (figure 18). The alligator on the original cover could be seen behind the pasted one, and the cut-off body of the alligator ended abruptly too close to the spine. The cover looked sloppy. At the eleventh hour, I redid the whole cover making two paintings: the background and a separate alligator with water hyacinths to camouflage the trouble spot near the spine (figure 19).

By the time the cover was finalized, the realistic alligator in his natural habitat, at the zoo, and in National Geographic *photos had turned into a caricature, M'sieur Cocodrie.*

One important lesson I've learned over the years is that my illustrations improve as I get deeper into the book, and so, because it is so important, I should do the cover last or plan from the beginning to do it a second time.

For some unhappy reason, I almost always have to do all of my "final" illustrations twice. I call the second run my "finalies."

In one of the Gingerbread Boy illustrations, I was just about to put the last touch of paint to paper when my husband, looking over my shoulder, said, "That shrimper is rowing! You'll be the laughingstock of every Cajun fisherman in Louisiana — you paddle *a pirogue!" I started over.*

READING LIST

1) Picture-Book World *by Bettina Hurlimann*
2) The Art of Art for Children's Books *by Diana Klemin*
3) The Illustrated Book *by Diana Klemin*
4) Illustrators of Children's Books *by Mahoney and Viguers*
5) American Picturebooks from Noah's Ark to the Beast Within *by B. Bader*
6) Writing with Pictures *by Uri Shulevitz*
7) The Telling Line *by Douglas Martin*
8) Children and Books *by Zena Sutherland and May Hill Arbuthnot*
9) Literature and the Child *by John Warren Stewig*
10) The Oxford Companion to Children's Literature *by Carpenter and Prichard*

Figure 1: The density of the dots create the sense of space as well as mass and line.

Figure 2 : The outline of this sphere and its shadow are not delineated by a line, and the values therein are not created by tone but by intersecting line.

Figure 3: Linear perspective is the study of the natural phenomenon where objects decrease in size as they recede farther back in space.

The seven classifications of value

1. The highlight
2. the light planes
3. the half tones
4. the cast shadows
5. reflected light
6. the dark planes
7. core of shadow

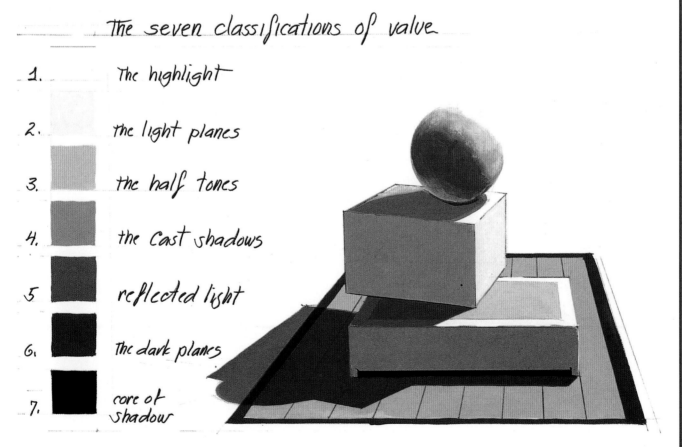

Figure 4: Value refers to the relation of a color to black and white and all the grays in between. In order to change the value of a color, we must mix it with something lighter or darker than itself.

Figure 5: Color perspective is the expression of distance and space by the addition of air color to pictorial elements. The more air color is added, the further in distance objects appear.

Figure 6: In this illustration, red and green are used as subject colors, and a warm gray is the air color. The subject colors are reduced in intensity by the air color as they recede into the distance.

Figure 7: Symmetrical compositions are usually static, yet can have a formal elegance. Asymmetrical compositions of the same subject usually hold more interest and allow the artist greater creativity in the organization of pictorial elements.

Figure 8: These pictures illustrate scale by showing a similar rock in each sketch, in combination with two differing human attributes; in turn, each sketch presents the viewer with a completely different sense of scale.

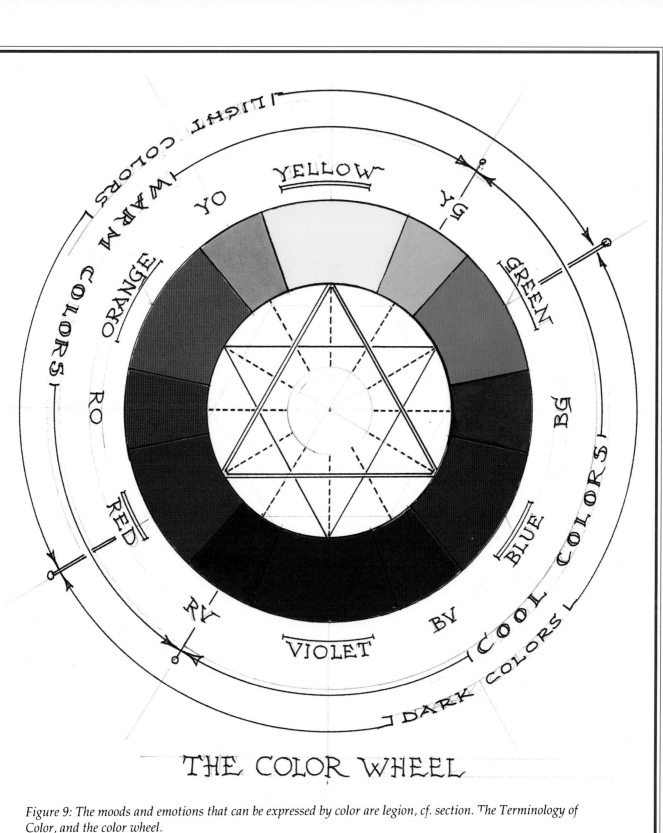

THE COLOR WHEEL

Figure 9: The moods and emotions that can be expressed by color are legion, cf. section. The Terminology of Color, and the color wheel.

Figure 10: *Jean Cassels' sketches are done in pencil on graphics 360, 100 per cent rag translucent marker paper.*

Figure 11: Jean Cassels checks her thumbnail sketch for color and does a larger color sketch, then mixes her colors to begin the painting.

Figure 12: Jean Cassels' finals are done on Arches 140-lb. hot-pressed, watercolor paper using gouache. She lays in large washes and goes from the general to the specific. In this book, **Prairie Dogs,** *the last thing to do was prairie-dog whiskers!*

Figure 13: Emily Arnold McCully keeps her sketches loose until the very last minute, submitting dummies that require a lot of imagination to interpret.

Figure 14: Emily Arnold McCully never uses color until the finish stage, so there remain a great many problems to solve.

Illustration by Emily Arnold McCulley from YOU LUCKY DUCK © 1988 Emily Arnold McCulley. Used by permission of Western Publishing Company, Inc.

Figure 15: This was the cover that was on the dummy of
The Show Must Go On *when Emily Arnold McCully first submitted it to Golden Books.*

Figure 16: This is the cover that was printed when Golden Books published the book several years later.

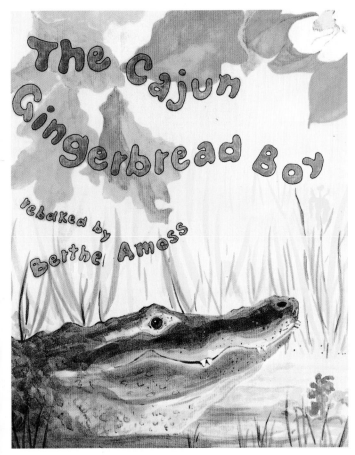

Figures 17: Berthe hand-printed the title in letters made to look like gingerbread, but before the cover got to the printer, Ellen Friedman, the art director, changed her letters to far more legible ones in red.

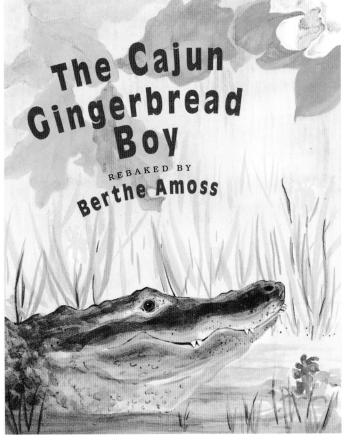

Figure 18: The alligator on the original cover could be seen behind the pasted one, and the cut-off body of the alligator ended abruptly, too close to the spine.

Figure 19: By the time the cover was finalized, the realistic alligator in his natural habitat, at the zoo, and in National Geographic photos had turned into a caricature, M'sieur Cocodrie. The illustration is done in gouache on watercolor paper.

Figure 20: A big incident is not needed on every page of a picture book, as shown by this sequence of four pages in which night falls and sends Tom scurrying for the warmth and safety of home.

JOAN ELIZABETH GOODMAN

FIGURES 21 - 22

Figures 21 and 22: By transforming the girl Rita into the bear Amanda, the author made her subject at once more "cuddly" and more universal.

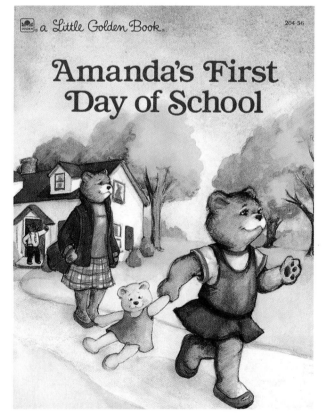

Figure 23: Knowing a great illustrator can help you get your story published, as shown by this stunning picture by Leonard Weisgard, a friend of author Jan Wahl.

MARY GRACE EUBANK

FIGURE 24

Figure 24: Golden Books editors remembered their shape book series and decided to die-cut the book in the shape of a schoolbus. So The Flying Schoolbus was born!

KATHY ALLERT

FIGURE 25

Figure 25: The drawings in the author's book dummy were essential to give meaning to her text — for instance, by showing the growth of a frog from an egg, while her text merely pointed out that changes were taking place.

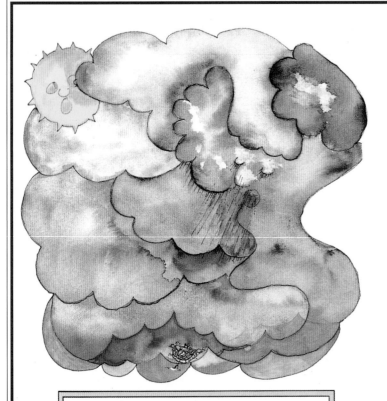

"The sky turned dark; the wind began to wail and whine. It was Bellowing Bertha being born! She breathed and blew, she groaned and grew and howled and yowled."

Figures 26 and 27: In this tall tale, a hurricane, Bellowing Bertha, is personified. The illustrations are done in pen and ink with watercolor on illustration board.

Oh woe, I'm feeling low!
Why I can hardly even blow!
Land's not so good for me-ee!
"Now I thought fast and threw out our ballast, and we glided to rest on the very next crest.

Chapter 7

SENDING IT OFF, SUBMITTING A MANUSCRIPT

A writer needs to know where to send his story. Which publisher will like it? The writer can learn by reading. He should spend time in bookstores and libraries, looking for children's books he likes. He should look, too, for books that are like the one he's written. When he likes a book, he should make note of the publisher's name. If you do this often enough, you will see trends and notice that every publisher has a kind of trademark; its books have a certain style. You should submit your manuscript to a publisher whose style appeals to you or is similar to your own.

If you are working on children's books, tell people what you are doing. Communicating with the people you know and networking can be important ways of identifying potential homes for your work. One writer told her husband about her story. He told a colleague at his law firm. The colleague had recently represented a publishing company. The writer sent her story to the publisher and sold her work the first time out.

If you know anyone with any connection to the publishing business, make use of the connection. Ask the acquaintance for names of people to whom you can submit your story. When writing to those people, mention your friend with the connection (if you have that person's permission, of course). It is said that Madeleine L'Engle's classic *A Wrinkle in Time* was rejected by more than twenty publishers before it was picked up by Farrar, Straus as a favor to the author's mother!

It is, however, important to send your story to an

Case History (Berthe)

I wrote and illustrated two picture books for Ursula Nordstrom, but when I showed her my third, a wordless story called By the Sea, *she said she had one wordless story on her list already.*

I took By the Sea *to Susan Hirshman. She turned it down nicely: "I'm sure someone will publish it," she said. "Who?" I asked, and she gave me five publisher's names.*

In the lobby of Macmillan's office building, there was a line of public telephone booths, separated by low walls. I went into one and called Viking, the first name on Susan's list. I was told to send my manuscript in like everyone else. "But I'm only in New York today!" I said.

"I couldn't help hearing you," said a woman in the next booth after I'd hung up. "Why don't you try Alvin Tresselt at Parents? I used to work for him and he's very nice."

I dialed the number and got an appointment. Alvin took By the Sea *and subsequently five more books, but who was the woman in the telephone booth? All I could tell the people I came to know and like at Parents was that she was a curly-headed blonde in a large coat. They were puzzled, but I always thought she was my guardian angel.*

"appropriate" publisher. The rejection of E.B. White's classic *Charlotte's Web* was legendary at Golden Books. If White had been doing his research, he would have known that Golden Books was not the place for literary fiction for preteens. Genius is not enough!

The publications entitled *Literary Market Place* (*LMP*) and *Children's Writer's and Illustrator's Market* contain good information about publishers' areas of specialization, names of key personnel, addresses and telephone numbers, and may include other important facts, such as submission policies. These books may be available in the reference section of your library. Many publishers' listings in *LMP* include the names and whereabouts of editors. A submission should always be addressed to a particular editor. Her name should be spelled correctly, and her title should be current. You can confirm this information by telephone.

The manuscript should be presentable before you send it. It should be carefully typed and double-spaced. As you type, check the spelling and usage of each word.

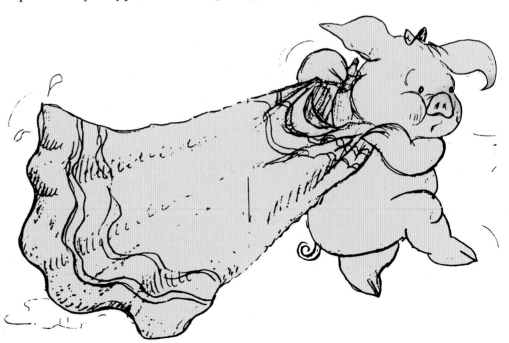

Check your punctuation. Neatness is not as vital in a book dummy. But a dummy should always be accompanied by a cleanly typed manuscript. If you have a good agent, she will not want to show a publisher anything but your best, most carefully written work.

Before mailing your manuscript, research the publisher's submission policies. One source of information is *Children's Writer's and Illustrator's Market*. Some publishers require query letters before submission. A query letter describes your story, its intended audience, its theme and format. It also introduces you and your special background to the editor. If your letter piques an editor's interest, she may invite you to submit the full manuscript.

Your letter should also suggest the "flavor" of your manuscript. Be careful, however. A whimsical tone may help set the mood for your original fairy tale; a letter in verse may give a taste of your rhyming text. But a query letter is still essentially a business letter, and it must contain some strictly business information: the length and genre of your story, your target age group, whether illustrations are needed, the "message" you hope to send young readers, your commercial "hook," and your reasons for writing to *this* publisher. The "hook" is some commercially appealing factor that tells the editor your book will sell.

An editor should be able to find some common-sense knowledge of publishing facts in your letter. Only an amateur describes a story as written for two- to ten-year-olds; no story appeals equally to toddlers and preteens. Don't say you've written a manuscript for a 43-page picture book. You should know that books are printed and bound in multiples of 16 pages, and so your manuscript should fill 32 or 48 book pages (with an allowance for front matter) and be structured accordingly.

You should also describe your actual experience with children. Trumpet your work as a teacher, counselor, or day-care

Case History (Eric)

A dummy can be an important visual aid, even if you do not end up illustrating the book. Nancy Buss, a writer, had been a commercial illustrator. When I received her manuscript for Ready, Set, Grow *(figure 25), it was accompanied by a dummy containing her skillful pencil drawings. The drawings were essential to give meaning to her text — for instance, by showing the growth of a chick inside the egg while her text merely pointed out that changes were taking place in the shell. Though Nancy's illustration style was not quite "right" for Golden Books, her drawings showed me what the book was about, and I was able to pass those ideas along to the art director, who gave them to the illustrator so that she could give true expression to Nancy's intent.*

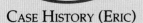

Case History (Eric)

Presentation matters when you are submitting a manuscript or book dummy. Though your dummy can contain simple stick-figure drawings and text, you may want to do something more elaborate, depending on your subject matter. For instance, the illustrator Amye Rosenberg once prepared a dummy to illustrate her idea for a book about colors. Each two-page spread "taught" a different color by incorporating an important scenic element in that color. Amye's dummy contained basic black-and-white drawings, but she added the dominant color to each spread with bright colored pencils or markers. When I reviewed this submission, I found that the addition of color helped convince me that Amye's color sense would add a special dimension to the book. I could see her point, and Lily Pig's Book of Colors *was born.*

worker. Any education you've had in writing for children — courses, workshops, seminars, group memberships — demonstrate commitment and some knowledge. Stress *any* prior publication of your writing — local magazines, trade or professional journals, campus newspapers. Any prior publication increases your credibility with publishers by letting them know that someone before them has liked your writing well enough to publish it. Experience as a parent or grandparent is common but worth mentioning. Keep your letter brief and to the point — two or three short paragraphs should suffice. If you feel you must write a longer letter, try not to exceed one page.

Here are two things *not* to say in your letter to publishers:

"I wrote the story for my children/grandchildren, and when I read it to them, they just loved it." Publishers justifiably feel that any child would love the experience of being held close by a beloved adult and read a story that was written just for him — this kind of puffery shows your qualities as a caregiver more than it demonstrates the quality of your writing.

"If you like this story, I have a whole series based on the same characters/theme/idea." Publishers find this notion frightening. They need to like *one* story first, and you're putting the cart before the horse by trying to sell the others before the first has a home. Publishers may also think that your expectations are unrealistic and that you won't be satisfied with the publication of just one of your stories. Your first submission needs to stand alone. This is true despite the fact that generally a publisher wants to find a writer who will be good for more than one book.

Many manuscripts go astray when they are submitted "over the transom," that is, without a prior query and without a green light from an editor. Merely adding an editor's name to the outside of the envelope will not necessarily solve your problem; publishers have procedures for tracking which manuscripts they've asked to see. Even with an editor's name, an unsolicited manuscript may end up on the stack of manuscripts processed by the company's "slush" readers. These readers plow through the work of hopeful writers who have not researched the company's submission policies. Often, slush readers can give manuscripts little more than a cursory glance.

The "slush" readers are

Case History (Eric)

It is important to put an individual's name on your letters and submissions. Years ago, after a boss of mine left Golden Books, I "inherited" her office and part of her list of projects. The mailroom continued routing her mail to me as well, assuming, I suppose, that some of it would be for me under the new circumstances. One day an envelope addressed to my predecessor arrived in my "in" box. I opened it up and found a dummy and manuscript that charmed me. It sounds farfetched, but I know that if the author had not written my predecessor's name on the envelope, I would never have seen How Things Grow *(figure 25) and would never have published it. And if I had never published that book, I would never have pursued the same author's* The Littlest Christmas Elf *through several revisions and eventual publication. But try to send manuscripts only to people who are still on staff — you may not have the same good fortune as Nancy Buss.*

the people who most likely will evaluate your query letter and manuscript, so you should know something about your first "audience." These readers are often entry-level workers called editorial assistants. They are usually young, college-educated people with a love of books and the ambition to move into positions as editors. They want the opportunity to discover and develop writers of "their own," for that is the best way for them to demonstrate their ability and move ahead in their careers. Even solicited manuscripts are most often read by these eager people, who are hired to do all the "drudge" work their busy bosses lack time to do.

For an editorial assistant, reading manuscripts is just one of many tasks. Other duties include answering phones, typing letters and manuscripts, proofreading and trafficking galleys, checking sketches, final artwork, and proofs, and writing reports on projects the boss has already signed up. The time-consuming process of reading and evaluating manuscripts with only a slight chance of acceptance seems unrewarding and unimportant. Still, the higher-ups often emphasize the importance of this work, and the fear of passing up a diamond among the dross is palpable and provides incentive. Bernette Ford, a top editor for years and now publisher of Cartwheel Books for Scholastic, used to allay assistants' fear of missing a gem by saying, "Don't worry; if it's really good, *someone* will publish it." And the law of averages suggests that she was right.

Thus, these readers, like most editors, *want* to find something publishable in the slush pile. You can make an overwhelmed reader sit up and take notice in two ways: through the quality of your work, and through the professionalism of your presentation. Spelling every word in your letter and manuscript correctly and putting the correct punctuation in the right places are rarer accomplishments than you might think. They make reading your work that much easier and more pleasant, and make you appear that much more credible as a candidate for furthering the literacy of young people.

If you retain an agent, he or she will handle all your submissions. But you must endure a similar submission process to find an agent. Seeking an agent is very much like seeking a

"It's a neat idea for a book, Mr. James, but there's way too many big words."

Drawing by Shanahan; © 1994 The New Yorker Magazine, Inc.

Case History (Eric)

A caveat about agents: An agent may adversely affect your relation-ship with a publisher. The best agents try to balance their clients' needs with the realities of the publishing business. The worst indulge their clients' excesses and are willing to trade short-term "victories" for long-term damage to their clients' credibility. I once acquired a fancy, high-profile picture book from an author-illustrator with whom I had worked only on simpler projects. I was going out on a limb and taking Golden Books with me — the book was a bit offbeat, and the author had never before undertaken as elaborate a project. Given the risk involved, our production department began to doubt whether we could afford to put a paper dust jacket over the full-color, glossy binding. The artwork was due the same week this controversy erupted; the artist wanted the dust jacket and decided to withhold her artwork until we would promise it to her. Her agent, rather than counseling her to do the professional thing, as well as the contractually required thing, by delivering her artwork, abetted her in withholding it. Though the book was finally published (with dust jacket) to some acclaim, it was the first and last time we ever did a splashy picture book with that author.

publisher. Agents are listed in *Literary Market Place*.

There are pros and cons to retaining an agent. The pluses include the agent's specialized knowledge of publishers and their needs and his familiarity with industry practices. For instance, an agent will know when William Morrow is launching a new imprint directed at toddlers and will get your story about play school to the appropriate editor more promptly than you could.

The drawbacks include his cut of your earnings (the present industry standard is 15-25 percent) and the fact that you may find yourself in competition with other authors he represents. Say that you have written a book about dinosaurs and so has another author represented by the same agent. The agent will not submit both stories to an editor interested in dinosaur books. Rather, the agent may send the manuscript he likes best or the one by the author whose name can fetch the bigger advance.

For years, many literary agents were reluctant to take on children's authors, thinking the return too slight. Now that children's books are bread-and-butter for many publishers, agents are eager to sign them up and many children's authors are represented. However, having an agent is not a prerequisite to becoming a published author. Many fine writers have done well without agents. Beverly Cleary is a notable example; she wrote and sold the first *Ramona* book on her own.

Publishers used to frown on simultaneous submissions, which means submitting the same work to more than one publisher at a time. Publishers wanted to be sure they were being offered properties exclusively before they went to the time and expense of reviewing the manuscripts and forming business plans. Nowadays, most publishers are prepared to see simultaneous submissions. However, you should inform the publisher that you are submitting your manuscript simultaneously at the time of your first communication.

The submission process may take a long time. Publishers try to control how long they hold manuscripts before responding. Doris Duenewald, who had a distinguished career as editor-in-chief at Grosset & Dunlap and later as publisher at Golden Books, used to encourage editors to review and respond to manuscripts in less than a month. "You can't tell me," she'd say, "that you don't know whether you like it the first time you read it." Still, not all editors share Doris' decisiveness, and the guidelines may bow to higher priorities.

Give the publisher about six weeks before you start following up. Don't be angry or threatening when you communicate with a publisher at this stage — that is a sure way to get a speedy rejection, regardless of the quality of your work. And always include a self-addressed, stamped envelope with your submission.

Some publishers have the courtesy to send each author a postcard stating that the publisher has received the manuscript, but many publishers do not. Consider enclosing a self-addressed, stamped postcard with your manuscript. Type something on the postcard to the effect that "We have received your manuscript and will be back in touch after we have completed our review." You may wish to leave a blank space where the editor can sign, or a box for her to check. But make it easy for the editor simply to pull the postcard out of your envelope and place it in her "out" box to be returned to you.

Remember, this is a business letter and should have a businesslike tone. Do not start your letter with the word "I"; emphasize the publisher's needs. For example: "Your series of easy-to-read books for first and second graders has been a boon to me and other teachers of my acquaintance. Now I have written a manuscript that you may wish to consider for inclusion in this series."

Reread your letter. How could you describe your story better? Reread your story. How could you rewrite it to be more appealing?

EXERCISE

After you have finished your manuscript, write out a query letter "selling" it to a publisher.

- *Describe your "idea": This portion should convey the commercial "hook," such as, "I have written a story about dinosaurs and divorce."*
- *Summarize the plot, briefly: "When Andy's parents divorce, he finds comfort in adventures with his imaginary dinosaur friend."*
- *Emphasize your theme: "This story emphasizes the power of imagination to help children cope with real-life situations."*
- *Define the genre, format, and age group: "This story, intended for readers in the grades K-2, is written in an easy-to-read style. It would be ideal in a softcover "I Can Read" format, 48 pages, with full-color illustrations."*
- *Describe yourself: "I am a teacher with ten years' experience introducing first and second graders to the fundamentals of reading."*

SELF-EDITING CHECKLIST:

- *Finish your manuscript.*
- *Put it away for a few days.*
- *Look at it objectively; then go to a bookstore and look for books that* look *like the book you think you've written. Note the names of the publishers of these books.*
- *Go to the library. Look up the names of the editors at these companies in LMP. Look up the publishers' submission policies in* Children's Writer's and Illustrator's Market.
- *Go home and draft your query letter; send one to each of the names on your list.*

SUGGESTED READING LIST

Each author or illustrator on this list chose to send different types of stories to different types of publishers. Look at the pairs of books below and see if you can understand why a different publisher was appropriate for each. Do you think the books with more mass appeal went to publishers better able to print and distribute large quantities of small, inexpensive books?

The Wheel on the Chimney *by Margaret Wise Brown*
Mister Dog *by Margaret Wise Brown*

Beauty and the Beast *illustrated by Mercer Mayer*
Just Me and My Dad *by Mercer Mayer*

Amelia Bedelia *by Peggy Parish*
My Little Golden Book of Manners *by Peggy Parish*

A Hole Is to Dig *by Ruth Krauss*
I Can Fly *by Ruth Krauss*

Eloise *illustrated by Hilary Knight*
Cinderella *by Hilary Knight*

Frog Went a-Courtin' *illustrated by Feodor Rojankovsky*
What Next, Elephant? *illustrated by Feodor Rojankovsky*

Chapter 8

REJECTION AND REVISION

By mailing your manuscript to the publisher, you kick-start the entire decision-making apparatus of the company. What happens to your book after it is submitted? It is the great paradox of children's publishing that although children must like your book if it is to become a classic, they don't have any say in getting it published. Adult editors have to like your book. Adult editors are sometimes asked whether they "use" children in their decision-making. The answer is no. That is because of commercial reality: Children do not buy children's books nor, with a few notable exceptions, do they review or give awards for children's books. Responsible educators and parents want to know that trained professionals are screening children's books for literary quality and age-appropriate content. Publishing companies want to know that the same professionals are screening submissions with an eye to commercial values.

It's a great start if one editor likes your story, though that may not be enough to make the publisher issue a contract. After forming a favorable impression of your work, the editor has to take the story to "editorial meeting" and get the other members of the editorial staff "on board." He has to persuade his superiors that the book demonstrates high quality and makes sense for the publisher's list. This process may involve detailed evaluation by other editors on the staff. He has to persuade the art director to try to give the book the right "look." People often ask what similarities exist between a career in publishing and a career in law, and there are many; but one of the strongest is the oral advocacy that must be done to persuade the "jury" (others in the company) to give the "client" (the book or author) a "break" (publication).

"Selling" the book to the company does not end at the editorial meeting. The process of getting the book ap-

Case History (Eric)

I was addressing a small writer's conference in Pennsylvania on the day my pet project — Isabelle Holland's The Christmas Cat — *was being presented at a sales conference. I phoned my office to find out how the presentation had gone. Apparently the presentation had generated a good bit of enthusiasm from the sales force until a salesman in the southeastern region objected to the cover. The cover depicted the main character in the foreground, with the Magi in the background and the Christmas star overhead. The salesman objected to the color of the cat — black! He told the group that black cats are associated with witchcraft in the South, and that no one in his region would buy a book on a religious theme if there were a black cat on the cover. Naturally, it was too late to change the book. But this story illustrates one of the many obstacles that may arise in "selling" the book to the publisher once it is already accepted.*

proved includes "selling" the business and production people on the idea that the book can be given a high-gloss production and still earn money for the company. Once the "package" is all together, but before publication, the editor must sell the book to the sales force! A sales conference is often held close to publication, and the fortunes of a book can rise or fall based on the sales staff's responses.

Rejection letters may be written by the editor at any of several stages in this process — after a first reading, after an editorial meeting, after a profit-and-loss analysis shows that the book would not generate sufficient revenue. But what does it mean when you receive a rejection letter? Most often it means that some editor did not like your book. Or it may not even mean anything as definite as that. It may mean that your book didn't "hit" that editor, didn't suddenly leap up as something he should spend time advocating or the company should go out of its way to produce. It doesn't mean that children will dislike your book or that your book is in some sense "bad." You have to learn to pick yourself up and start again. Send your manuscript to another house right away.

What is a rejection letter? Generally, it is a form letter that you receive in response to your query or as a cover letter with your returned manuscript. It will usually employ some cryptic and frustrating phrases in a lame attempt to explain why the publisher has chosen not to publish your story. However, you should know that publishers often use these time-honored formulae for a beneficent purpose — they don't want you to waste time altering your story in response to specific criticism when the manuscript may be just right for some other publisher.

The following stock phrases will tell you when you have received a form rejection letter:

"Your story is not right for our list at this time."

"We do not have a place on our list for your story."

"Our publishing list is filled up for the next several seasons."

"Sales data show that stories about the circus no longer sell."

90

That rationale holds if your story has any merit. An editor experiences a rare sinking feeling when reading a manuscript with not a single redeeming feature. In such a circumstance, an editor is very happy to have these stock phrases to coin anew. But don't assume that your manuscript falls into this category just because those old bromides appear in the letter you receive.

Try not to put too much pressure on the editor, or yourself, at the review stage. It may just be a waste of time and resources and merely serve to delay the inevitable rejection. If you get an in-person appointment with an editor, make your pitch and leave your work for the editor's leisurely review. Do not make the editor review your work while you sit looking on from the visitor's chair. Editors, like many people, don't like confrontation and in any event prefer to express themselves in writing. They may find it difficult to tell you to your face that they dislike your work, and therefore may ask to keep it for another reading. They may find it difficult to like your work *because* you're sitting there pressuring them to do so. Letting the editor relax with your work, by himself, may be the best way to get the most positive response.

All that a rejection letter really means, then, is that a particular editor on a particular day did not like your manuscript. Editors have only a few qualifications for their jobs — one is language skills; but the other more important requirement is taste. An editor does not have to have good taste to be a good editor— she merely has to have taste that reflects the aesthetic of her company and some segment of the buying public. Thus, the editor who acquired *The Toilet Book* by Jan Pienkowski recognized that small children like bathroom humor, that some parents pander to their children's baser preferences, and that her company could successfully manufacture and market novelty books. It wasn't an exercise in good taste, but it worked for the company and for a segment of the buying public.

CASE HISTORY (ERIC)

The most remarkable rejection I ever saw took place in a face-to-face meeting. Two entrepreneurs had an appointment to pitch a new children's-book character to the publisher and editor-in-chief of Golden Books. The character — a little alien or space creature — was poorly conceived and poorly drawn and showed almost no potential for exploitation as a book character. After feeling out the entrepreneurs with a few pointed remarks, the publisher said, "This proposal is no good."

Having been trained to worry about the feelings of people submitting work for review, I worried that the pair would express hurt or anger. But that isn't what happened at all. They said, "Thank you. We wanted to know if we were wasting our time with this project."

CASE HISTORY (BERTHE)

After four years of rejections, I finally "recognized" a good idea when my three-year-old had a temper tantrum because his nine-year-old brother had a birthday. I was about to go to New York, so I wrote Susan Hirshman at Harper & Row, to whom I had been submitting picture book manuscripts, asking for an appointment.

Charlotte Zolotow wrote back that Susan was no longer with them but that they would see me at eleven o'clock the day I requested.

Through sheer serendipity with some magic thrown in, I happened to see an announcement in Publishers Weekly, a magazine I didn't know existed, that Susan was at Macmillan. I wrote to her, and she gave me an appointment at ten o'clock the day I requested.

When she saw it, Susan liked my story and made a note in the margin. But she didn't take it, and I went on to my eleven o'clock appointment at Harper & Row. Charlotte liked my story, too, and brought me and it to Ursula Nordstrom, the formidable editor-in-chief of Harper & Row.

In reading It's Not Your Birthday, Ursula noticed Susan's note. "Who wrote this? Are you free to offer us this manuscript?" she asked.

"Susan Carr (Hirshman later)," I answered. "Yes, I'm free."

"Then, we'll take it." Ursula said the magic words, but I have never known whether she took it because she loved it or because she was angry that Susan had left Harper.

You can read several morals into this case history as I see it, but the most important is that persistence pays off. Second, the most marketable aspect of a picture book text is the uniqueness of your heartfelt idea behind it.

The following sample rejection letters summarize differing responses to the same manuscript. In other words, all rejection letters are not the same! Each of these letters calls for a different type of response.

> Dear Author:
>
> Thank you for sending your manuscript, Dolly's Busy Day, which we have read with interest. While your story has merit, we regret that we do not have a place for it on our list at this time. Perhaps another publisher will have a different response.
>
> Your manuscript is returned herewith, with thanks for the opportunity to consider it.
> Sincerely,
>
> Ed Editor

This is a form rejection letter. You can tell because it says nothing specific about you or your story besides your name and title. You should put this letter aside and move on. Now consider the following letter:

Dear Author:

Thank you for sending your manuscript, Dolly's Busy Day, which we have read with interest. While the simple story is not quite right for our list, which is heavily weighted toward school-age children who can already read a little, we admired your tight plotting and sprightly dialogue. If you should ever decide to try your hand at a story in the easy-to-read genre, we would be most interested to see it.

Your manuscript is returned herewith, with regret. Thank you for the opportunity to consider it.
Sincerely,

Ed Editor

This letter is a "come-on." The editor clearly liked some very specific things about your writing and wants to see more. If you are not sure what the jargon means — for instance, the phrase "easy-to-read genre" — this is an opportunity to start a dialogue with the editor. Pick up the phone and call, or write a letter expressing your gratitude and interest in exploring possibilities on the editor's terms.

A less clear-cut situation may be presented by a letter such as the following:

Dear Author:

Thank you for sending your manuscript, Dolly's Busy Day, which we have read with interest. This story is not right for our list in its present form, though we enjoyed your tight plotting and sprightly dialogue. The simplicity of your manuscript is one of its virtues but is not in keeping with the tone of our picture book list, which emphasizes stories that will lend themselves to lavish illustration by award-winning artists and top-notch production values. If Dolly were a Victorian porcelain doll rather than a homemade ragdoll, her story might work better for us, especially with a few more episodes providing an opportunity to show rich settings and period detail.

If you should decide to rework your story along the lines mentioned above, we would be happy to take another look. Meantime, your manuscript is returned herewith, with thanks for the opportunity to consider it.
Sincerely,

Ed Editor

Case History (Eric)

Unless you are sure you have a contract, do not travel long distances to meet with an editor who has expressed an interest in seeing your work. I once received a telephone call from a woman who said she was going to be in New York the following week and had a proposal to discuss with me. The proposal sounded promising, so I made an appointment. Her proposal turned out to be terrible, and I told her the project was "not for us." The author then informed me angrily that she had traveled across country solely for this meeting. Now I felt badly that she had taken so much trouble only for a summary rejection. I offered a "second opinion" by another editor. My colleague corroborated my opinion, and being more tough-minded, showed the visitor the door.

Case History (Eric)

A "no" from a particular publisher does not have to be forever. When I was still an editorial assistant, a rising illustrator submitted a picture book dummy that I loved. This story about a family of performing bears was a perfect fit with my theatrical background. At the editorial meeting, the consensus was that the project was "not for us." Just a few years later, I had progressed from an assistant with no power to a full editor with control of my own list of books. When presented with the challenge of developing a series of books that would be truly "special," I set about soliciting the work of writers and artists whom I admired. One of these was Emily Arnold McCully. Emily sent in the story about the performing bears, which I easily recognized from years before. Now I could act on my desires, and I jumped to get The Show Must Go On *for my list. (See figures 15 and 16)*

Now the author has a quandary. She wrote about a homemade ragdoll because she had such a doll when she was a girl and wanted to show children that humble things could be beautiful and lovable. She feels hurt because some big-city editor has rejected *her* Dolly. This writer may put the letter away and keep trying with the story in its present form.

But wait. There might be another approach. A story employing the suggested elements might imply your original theme by playing up the "bird in the gilded cage" aspects of the porcelain doll's existence. Of course, this approach would work only if the writer felt truly comfortable with the editor's ideas — *merely* writing to suit the editor may not work unless the author has a genuine response to the suggestion. In the end, the benefit may be that the writer has two manuscripts that work rather than one — the frilly doll story for the publisher who wants that approach, and the plain one for another publisher. (One caveat: The author may want to be careful about competing with herself, and may also want to be wary about being typecast as the person who writes the doll stories.)

The lesson to be learned here is to read your rejection letters. Ordinarily, they will be of the form type typified by sample number one above, and you may not feel that the publisher has even read your story. However, if the letter contains any specific criticism or reaction to your story, it may not be a complete rejection, as in samples two and three. A busy editor rarely takes time to make an individual comment on your work unless it aroused her interest.

An editor may ask you to revise "on spec." This phrase means that if you revise according to the editor's

instructions and he is satisfied with your changes, your story may be published. If your changes are not satisfactory and your book is not published, you will get nothing for your trouble. If you are revising on spec, be on your best behavior. The editor will be looking to see how you handle revisions. But he will also be interested in your attitude. Do you answer correspondence promptly? Are you cooperative? Are you willing to trust the editor? Can you articulate reasoned responses when you disagree? Publishing is a collaborative business. You should seem to be willing to work together to make a final product that will suit everyone's needs.

Case History (Eric)

Sometimes the author takes it upon himself to revise, without specific direction from an editor. Jan Wahl sent me his manuscript entitled Little Dragon's Grandmother. *Jan's writing style is subtle and poetic, and there was a false note somewhere in the story that I couldn't identify. I sent it back to Jan with the standard rejection language that the book was not "right" for us. Jan sent it back to me several times, having made a tiny adjustment each time. The last time he sent it, everything suddenly worked and I offered a contract for the book. Jan felt comfortable resubmitting his story to me, despite my repeated rejections, because he and I had an established working relationship. Do not try resubmitting if you have received a standard form rejection.*

By contrast, I wanted to publish Fran Manushkin's Beach Day *because of the descriptive artistry of her writing. She had taken as her model Margaret Wise Brown, and felt that the key to Brown's writing was the fact that she never had a word too many in her books. Fran kept cutting and cutting her manuscript in emulation of her model, until I had to plead with her to stop! Don't be afraid to revise to make your story work; but once it works,* stop.

Exercise

If you have received a personalized rejection letter along the lines mentioned in this chapter, try to revise your story to meet the editor's objections. How do you feel about the result? Is it still "your" story? Would you be able to live with its being published under your name?

If you have not received such a rejection letter, share your story with a writers' group or a trusted, experienced, published friend. Assure your readers that you want them to be absolutely honest and to provide constructive advice. Don't be defensive when you get feedback — in fact, it may be better to have your readers provide written responses. Decide if you agree with any of the criticism you receive, and try to revise your story accordingly if after reflection you can see your story from another point of view.

Revision, however, is a tricky business, and because you will seldom get two readers, professional or friends, who will agree, it is sometimes best not to revise until an editor has seen your original manuscript.

READING LIST

The following books were rejected prior to publication or significantly revised prior to final acceptance. Can you see why each work may not have been "right" for some publishers? Focus on subject matter, theme and tone.

A Wrinkle in Time *by Madeleine L'Engle*
Melly's Menorah *by Amye Rosenberg*
Time Train *by Paul Fleischmann*
Henry and Grudge *by Isabelle Holland*
Tim Kitten and the Red Cupboard *by Jan Wahl*
The Stratford Devil *by Claude C. Smith*

EXERCISE

Editors-in-training must learn to trust their instinct that something is "wrong" when it sets off a bell in their heads. You can develop this instinct, too, and use it to revise effectively even without an editor's input. Go through your manuscript carefully. Identify each and every spot that sounds "not right" to you. Now work to fix each of those spots, making sure the changes are true to the theme and tone of your story.

SELF-EDITING CHECKLIST

- *Review your manuscript thoroughly.*
- *Make sure you are expressing yourself as clearly as possible.*
- *Make sure you are not using too many words; eliminate all unnecessary adverbs and adjectives.*
- *Break up complex sentence structures; one thought per sentence is a good rule of thumb.*
- *Make sure that each thought flows logically from the one before it.*
- *Eliminate redundancies.*
- *Look for incorrect or poor word choices and replace them with more effective and appropriate words.*
- *Check for places where adding dialogue or describing a character's sensations would make the prose more alive.*

Chapter 9

Editors and Agents and What They Look For

---

*T*he true editor love to get mail. She relishes the thought of arriving at her office and finding a stack of brown envelopes, each containing a manuscript to read. Despite discouraging warnings you may have heard, editors want to find new writers. An editor dreams of discovering a talent whose work she can publish for the first time. It doesn't take much talent to solicit the work of well-known, award-winning artists like Barbara Cooney and Trina Schart Hyman. But an editor may prove her mettle by being the first to discover someone truly special. The challenge for the children's book writer is to mark himself as that special talent.

An editor opening your manuscript is looking for three things: talent, a publishable manuscript, and professionalism. Talent is difficult to define but can reveal itself in many ways. Basically, it is the special ingredient you add that makes your book about dinosaurs different from all the others on the market. A publishable manuscript is one that is well written and that has a "hook." Professionalism is shown in the neatness and correctness of your work, a businesslike approach to communications with the editor, promptness, and a cooperative spirit.

Talent may reveal itself in many different facets of your work. You may show talent by the way you narrow your subject. Let's say you're writing a book about dinosaurs. Choosing that tried-and-true topic shows no special talent. But maybe you've found a new slant on dinosaurs. If your book is nonfiction, you may have decided to write about a particular

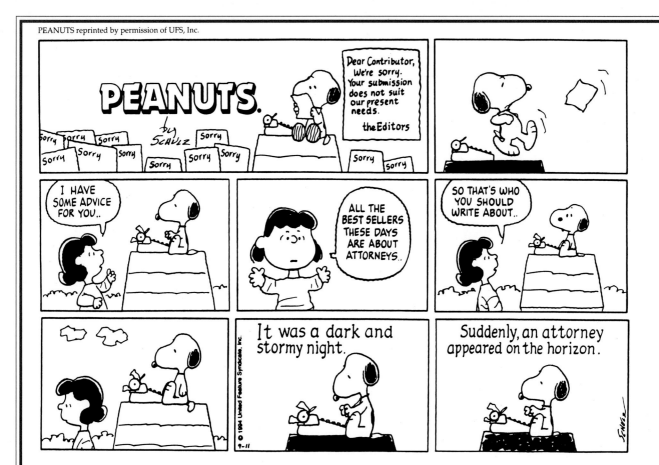

class or category of dinosaurs. If your story is fiction, perhaps you have chosen to use dinosaur characters for a good reason that relates to the theme of your story.

Still, no talent is as important as a talent for good writing. Writing for children — like writing for *anyone* — is an art. It is difficult and takes time and requires that the artist build his skills into a technique. This book is an attempt to help you do so by identifying the issues and breaking down the elements of the task at hand. But the important contribution comes from you and your refusal to be satisfied with your work until every sentence feels alive.

Consider the difference between these two sentences:

"One sunny day, Mary walked down the street."

"Mary felt the sun on her face as she hurried to town."

Most editors — most *readers* — would rather read a story about a character who feels things and expresses a sense of purpose with her actions. The first sentence could be written by anyone with a typewriter; the second shows a talent for characterization and storytelling.

However, good writing is not the only kind of talent that matters in writing for children. Judy Blume is an author whose writing shows a lot of rough edges and awkwardness. But Ms. Blume has an incomparable talent for accurately recognizing and depicting the true emotions of young people. Her stories may not be the most shapely, her prose not the most elegant, but her ability to penetrate the hearts and minds of young people is unique and has made her a popular and beloved author.

Reading aloud is a good test of your writing. Many children's books are read aloud, so the "sound" of your work is important. Is your text lively, mellifluous, interesting when you *say* it? Don't be surprised to learn that picture book editors test for these qualities by reading manuscripts aloud to themselves. It is a good sign if key phrases stick in the mind after the reader is finished. If you find yourself reciting little phrases out of context, you're probably succeeding. Keep in mind that children love to hear favorite stories again and again, and the memorable turn of phrase is one way to keep them wanting *your* story. Editors may have the same response.

Editors look for talent first because they are thinking beyond the manuscript at hand to a future relationship that may develop with the author. The most efficient and rewarding way for an editor to work is by establishing strong relationships with a core group of consistent writers. For the writer, becoming part of this group requires making sure that every manuscript you send reflects your best effort using your special abilities. There have been cases where a publisher rejected an author's manuscript but contacted her later and solicited other stories because of the talent shown in the first work.

Nevertheless, the best starting point for getting published is sending a publishable manuscript. A publishable manuscript is a well-written story with an interesting plot and a strong, universal theme. Like talent, plot is difficult to define; think of it as the thing that keeps the reader turning the pages. It is important that your story have all these features before you start sending it to editors. You can make sure by rereading it and analyzing it closely. Does it do all the things you want it to do? Does it communicate your message clearly?

You should not write "for the market." Only by writing from your inspiration can you demonstrate the spark — the "talent" — that distinguishes your work. Keep in mind, however, that an editor will be looking for a "hook" in your story. A *hook* is a proven commercial element that can be exploited in marketing your book. (*Marketing* means promoting and selling.) A commercial hook may be a tried-and-true subject, like dinosaurs. It may be a special focus on that subject, for

CASE HISTORY (ERIC)

When I think about stories that I wanted to accept on the spot, I recognize that the respective authors had a special talent for dialogue that was unexpected but childlike and true to the characters who spoke it. Each of these tiny moments felt "true" to me and touched my heart each of the dozens of times I read the texts during the production process. One such moment, in Jan Wahl's Let's Go Fishing!, *grabbed me from the first and grabs me still. A little boy and his grandfather are going fishing and begin by digging for worms. The little boy digs up only a few, because he likes to watch them crawl away. At last he says to his grandfather, "I can't fish with these… They are my friends." A writer's talent for dialogue may be like an actor's talent for improvisation: Try to imagine things your character might say, and don't stop at the obvious. Your dialogue needs to do two things — reveal character and move the plot. Revealing character is where your talent can shine if you try to write dialogue that has individuality and charm.*

instance, baby dinosaurs. It may be some special expertise that you can bring to the subject: Do you have access to new information about baby dinosaurs that has never been used in a children's book?

You can find your hook by visiting a library and looking at children's books on your subject. A survey will show you what books on the subject are being published and how your book differs from those on the market. If your book is not different or better, you may want to think about reworking it.

If you don't want to rework your book, think about other ways to make it more marketable. Start with yourself: What degrees do you have, what experience, what background with the subject matter? Then think about the people you know — any famous illustrators who might be willing to work on your project? There are numerous instances of a marginal manuscript being accepted because an established illustrator expressed interest in doing the pictures (see figure 23). Do you know a distinguished educator or scientist who would be willing to contribute a foreword to your book?

You need not be overly concerned if you don't have any hooks of this kind; just be aware that if you *do* have one, it may make publication an easier goal to reach. Editors are practiced in the art of identifying and exploiting the hook buried in the author's manuscript. But *you* have to hook the editor. Your talent may be one hook. But try to think of other features that make your work commercial, especially if you are writing a picture book, where the hook may be more subtle than in nonfiction books. Is the book about stepfamilies, middle children, birthdays? Does it take place on Christmas or Hanukkah or during World War II? Take stock of all the features of your story and try to play up the most engaging of them in presenting your manuscript for publication.

Don't confuse having a

Case History (Eric)

Dinah L. Moché is the author of many popular astronomy books for children. The allure of stars and planets is one of the hooks that draws readers to her work. Another is the author herself. Not only is she a credentialed professor of astronomy, but Dr. Moché is familiar with NASA resources and participates in many official space-related activities for young people. This personal involvement means that the author's research is completely up-to-date. Just as important from the editor's viewpoint, the author knows the NASA archives and the pictorial material they contain. Her contact with children means that she knows exactly what information her readers will find most interesting. Dr. Moché, through her expertise and activities, is able to "choreograph" an entire project in a way that appeals to editors and children alike.

hook with being original. Your baby
dinosaur book need not be the only one on
the market. In publishing, imitation is truly
the sincerest form of flattery; a publisher
will never mind an opportunity to duplicate a rival's success.

In addition to your talent and your
manuscript, a publisher will be looking
for your professionalism. Professionalism
has several aspects, beginning with your
approach to your craft. You should
appear to know language and how to use
it. You are presenting yourself as a
wordsmith. From your query letter on, every word you send the editor should be correctly spelled and used. Double-check your punctuation.

You should also demonstrate a professional attitude by taking a businesslike
approach in communications with your editor. At the outset, be pleasant but not familiar. When criticism is offered, try not to be emotional in your response — your editor is
trying to improve your story, not attacking you personally. If you feel that you cannot
respond to comments without getting angry or upset, ask for a little
time to digest the criticism, then respond in writing if you do not
trust yourself to speak in a measured way. If you feel that your
intent or expression is being misunder-
stood, try to explain yourself in a
rational manner,
and by all means
stick to your
guns if anyone
suggests changes
with which you
do not agree. But
be cool in stating
your resolution.
No one likes to
deal with a
prima donna —
and no one gets to *be* a prima donna
unless they've already been published *and* successful.

Try to remember that you are
not the only author on the editor's
list. The editor is working on a wide
variety of projects at any time and
will not appreciate your making
excessive demands on his time and
attention. On the other hand, you
need to communicate when appropri-

EXERCISE

*Identify the hook in each of the following books.
Remember that there may be more than one.*

The Polar Express *by Chris Van Allsburg*
The Nutcracker *illustrated by Maurice Sendak*
Number the Stars *by Lois Lowry*
Forever *by Judy Blume*
Like Jake and Me *by Mavis Jukes*

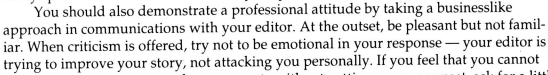

CASE HISTORY (ERIC)

*Your editor is your primary contact at the publishing
company and the person with the greatest stake in seeing
your book succeed. Always respect the editor's position
and interest in your success, and do not go around him
when you feel you are not getting the response you want.
I once accepted a picture book manuscript from a new
author with strong ideas about the illustrations. The
characters in the story were based on the author's own
children and grandchildren, and she wanted to supply
family photographs for the illustrator to copy. I explained
that the illustrator also had a vision and an important
role to play in the creation of the book, and that therefore
the author's suggestion was inappropriate. The author
then wrote directly to the art director about her ideas.
The art director angrily asked me to get the author off her
back. I rebuked the author for her conduct and asked her
to communicate with me if she had any further problems
with anything I told her. She sent an apologetic note, but
I never worked with her again.*

ate and necessary, and the occasional note or phone call to keep in touch can be pleasant. It can also stimulate a dialogue about present and future projects.

Above all, *always* be polite. Authors often feel slighted when promotion and advertising are less elaborate then they had hoped or when sales are disappointing. Such responses are natural. But the situations themselves are almost never of the editor's making. Most often, the editor will share your disappointment. Try to resist the urge to call up and yell. You will only upset yourself and others, and you may spoil your chances of working with that editor or publisher in the future.

Finally, a publisher may look at the people you know. The publishing world is really more like a small village in which most people know each other. It should be no secret that many authors are published because they know editors or other publishing professionals. People are published because they are related to well-known authors or illustrators or have a promise that such well-known people will somehow contribute to the book. If you have published before with another publisher, the new editor may check up on you with acquaintances at your first house — another reason to be on your best behavior.

Do not feel discouraged if you don't know anybody who can help you get published. Your talent, manuscript, and professionalism are the most effective ways to recommend yourself to publishers, and it is in your control to develop and polish those things into attractive bait with which to lure and hook publishers. If you are worried by your lack of contacts, you can try to fix that, too. Start to attend writers' conferences and workshops where editors and agents will be in attendance.

Make friends with your local booksellers and librarians. They will be interested in what you're doing, and most have publishing contacts. In the last chapter of this book, we have asked various people in the children's book field to give you advice.

Progress Checklist

Review your manuscript carefully, searching for hooks you can emphasize to editors. Pay special attention to features in the following categories:
- *Subject matter: Do you have a "high interest" or "hot" topic?*
- *Setting: Does your story take place in an interesting time period or unusual place?*
- *Characters: Are your animal characters a popular type of animal, your humans based on beloved "types"?*
- *Author/illustrator: What makes you an especially apt person to handle this topic?*

READING LIST

The following books all have the spark of life that makes a book irresistible to editors and readers alike. Study the authors' characterizations, dialogue, and language to discern just what it is that grabs the reader.

The Adventures of Tom Sawyer *by Mark Twain*
Heidi *by Johanna Spyri*
Sarah, Plain and Tall *by Patricia MacLachlan*
The Story of Babar *by Jean de Brunhoff*
Madeline *by Ludwig Bemelmans*
Eloise *by Kay Thompson*

SELF-EDITING CHECKLIST

- *Check that you have a distinctive approach to your topic.*
- *Analyze your writing to see that it is "alive."*
- *Do you show what your characters feel rather than merely tell what they do?*
- *Is your dialogue individual and in character?*
- *Does your text sound good when read aloud?*
- *Make sure that your plot is a logical, interesting sequence of events.*
- *Verify the presence of two or three hooks you can push in selling the manuscript to editors.*
- *Make a list of people you know who have some connection to the publishing world. Contact these people as appropriate.*
- *Edit your correspondence to editors for tone and content; be polite, businesslike, and thorough, but succinct.*

Chapter 10

IS THERE LIFE AFTER PUBLICATION?

"*I*f only I could get my books published!"

Writers are often so intent on that goal that they forget that publication is only the birth of a book, the beginning of its life.

After you have done your best to create a book that satisfies you, and it has been accepted by a publisher, your book's fate, either a long life or a quick, unhappy death, is in the hands of others.

Writers and illustrators may find it so difficult to break into the children's book market that they overlook the reality that if the publisher's sales force doesn't love it, reviewers ignore it or give it a bad review, booksellers don't order it, librarians do not recommend it, teachers find no merit in it, parents don't want to pay for it, the book will have a hard time even reaching the hands of a child.

And then, of course, there is the child, your reader and the ultimate judge of your book. If a child does not like a book, it doesn't matter what all of those other people think, say, or do. In the immortal words of Paul Hazard, "What precocious skill they [the

children] have for skipping paragraphs, pages, whole chapters... We always hesitate, we men, to throw a book in the wastebasket because it bores us... Our habits are formed and we are so resigned that it seems as though a little boredom is necessary to real admiration. So we keep on courageously, waiting for the consoling page, even reproaching ourselves for our yawns. But the children are ruthless... they cannot be made to believe that a book which displeases them should please them...." (*Books, Children and Men*, Paul Hazard.)

You needn't be discouraged by the distance between book and child; you will find that the more you work with the people involved with children's books, the more you will see their eagerness to help you.

We all share with you a love and knowledge of children's books and an interest in making your book as attractive as possible to readers.

Throughout this book, we have tried to show you through case histories, advice, and exercises how to write to the best of your ability and how to self-edit your work so that when you send your manuscript to an editor, you will be confident that your book is publishable.

In this chapter, we have invited editors, reviewers, librarians, agents, teachers, booksellers, and writers to tell you what they look for when choosing books.

Listen well! Their words are golden and will give you invaluable insights into your own work.

SUSAN LARSON

Susan Larson is the book editor of The Times-Picayune, *New Orleans's daily paper. She has also been manager of the bookstore at the University of New Orleans and is the author of several books.*

As book editor of *The Times-Picayune*, I see thousands of books come across my desk each year. Many are children's books to be assigned to one of our three children's-book columnists. But as the mother of two eager young book lovers, I can't resist looking at them myself, and I often write about my favorites. Here are a few thoughts about working with your local press, and finding your place in the local literary community, and creating wonderful books for children.

First off, let them know you're there. Drop a line introducing yourself and your project when you move to a new place, or when your paper changes book editors. You could start by letting an editor or children's news reporter know that you've sold a book, and then remind them again before it comes out. Once your book has been published, call to be sure that it has been received, or send a copy yourself. But if you send your own book, be sure not to enclose a letter; very often, in the rush of opening many book cartons each day, accompanying paperwork becomes lost or separated. Send letters under separate cover. Make sure that you let local media know well in advance of any scheduled autographings or personal appearances for inclusion in community calendars. And read or call your newspaper to make sure you address the information to the proper individual.

Be creative in terms of off-the-book-page publicity. If your book has an unusual angle, a local connection, or a holiday tie-in, point that out. Remember that newspapers may cover library or school appearances.

Take criticism gracefully, for it is usually well meant. After all, most writers enter the reviewing world because they love books. And remember, not every book will be reviewed due to space limitations.

Find a writers' support group and attend meetings. Meet as many teachers of children's literature as you can. Make friends with librarians and booksellers. They can become powerful advocates, and remember, they are the first people who will be asked to buy your book!

Support your fellow writers by attending readings and autographings. Go to every literary festival, conference, every literary event that you can. When one writer benefits, the entire literary community benefits.

Remember that reviewing children's picture books calls for a unique set of talents, and not many reviewers are equally well versed in critical approaches to art and text. Some reviewers naturally gravitate toward color and style, and others toward a lyrical text. But most are drawn by a unique and appealing combination of word and image. It's an intensely personal and idiosyncratic reaction.

Reviews of children's books should answer several basic questions. First, I think the reviewer has a responsibility to render an opinion. Is it a good book, a bad book, a mediocre book? Is it worth the money? (As children's books become increasingly expensive, I think this is a real consideration.) Is this book by an established author/illustrator or a new one? Is the author breaking new ground? Does the author/illustrator deliver in terms of character, plot, illustration? What lessons, what values, does a child take away from this book?

My greatest asset in my work as book review editor is that I am a reader and a lover of books. I never tire of books, and I am always looking out for something new and wonderful. And my second greatest asset is being a parent, which makes a person look at the whole world a little differently, and that includes the world of books.

I want my children to have books that are beautiful, like Bill Joyce's lovely paean to spring, *Bently and Egg*. I want them to have books that will instruct them in the sometimes sad ways of the world, like *The House That Crack Built*. I want books to demonstrate the possibilities that are open to them, like *Amazing Grace*, by Mary Hoffman, illustrated by Caroline Bunch. I want books to make them laugh, like the wonderful, witty poetry of Jack Prelutsky, which should be a part of every childhood. I want books that show the diversity and strength of families, like *Free to be a Family*, by Marlo Thomas & Friends. I look for books that will deepen the mystery of life, like Chris Van Allsburg's remarkable *The Widow's Broom*, as well as illuminate it, like Michael Bedard's wonderful book *Emily*, with lovely illustrations by Barbara Cooney, a book that gives a child's eye-view of a great American poet. I want books that celebrate the joy of reading, like Patricia Polacco's *The Bee Tree*, in which a wise grandfather describes the sweetness to be found in books. "Such things… adventure, knowledge and wisdom. But these things do not come easily: You have to pursue them. Just like we ran after the bees to find their tree, so you must also chase these things through the pages of a book!"

The very best children's books make the chase a lifelong passion.

ELIZABETH GORDON

Elizabeth Gordon is editor-in-chief and publisher of Disney Press/Hyperion Books for Children.

What I look for in a good children's book is, in many ways, no different from what I look for in my own personal reading. The most important ingredients are good, believable characters, a plot that makes inherent sense and that carries the reader along to a satisfying conclusion, and fine, well-crafted writing. A unique voice and emotional depth makes a book memorable. Picture book writing needs to sparer and more evocative than the writing in a novel since far fewer words must convey the story and/or mood. In either case, the complexity of the writing, plot and characters should have a natural relationship to each other and to the age of the reader for which the book is intended.

EDEN ROSS LIPSON

Eden Ross Lipson is children's book editor of The New York Times *and the author of* Parent's Guide to the Best Books for Children.

The proper analogy to a great children's book is probably opera, because in memory the words and music are inseparable. In fine children's books, the words and the illustrations are inseparable and illuminate each other. The reader should be able to read the text aloud without stumbling over inappropriate or ambiguous punctuation and typography.

MARY PRICE ROBINSON

A former employee of The Savile Bookstore in Washington, D.C., and a sales rep for Random House, Mary Price Robinson is the owner of Beaucoup Books, which she opened in the fall of 1983. Mary Price is president of New Orleans-Gulf South Booksellers Association.

It seems that each year more and more children's books are being published, and as the owner/buyer of a bookstore with limited selling space, I must carefully choose the books that will take up that space.

I suppose my first consideration is whether or not I immediately *like* the book. That is, when I look at sample pages (or even catalog copy), am I drawn to the visual appeal of the illustrations as well as the story? I think about whether or not my customers will see and appreciate what I do. Will parents and children react as I have to a particular title and be excited about it?

When selecting picture books for young children, I prefer a fairly simple, concise text and interesting illustrations, either vibrant or softer and more muted. I want a book that will stand out on the shelf and for one reason or another attract the eye of the customer.

Early reader and young adult book purchases are driven more by customer demand and recommendations from sales reps.

I prefer more classic books such as *Charlotte's Web*, yet I stock the "hot" new series as well as books that teachers might assign for class. In general, these books seem to have a longer shelf life than picture books; maybe because there seem to be fewer of them published.

COLEEN SALLEY

Coleen Salley is Professor of Children's Literature at the University of New Orleans and a professional storyteller, known throughout the publishing world.

I want in my children's books, be they picture books or novels, just exactly what I want in my adult books. I want to be entertained. But because I am educated, older, and world traveled, I am not that easily entertained.

A story told in words or pictures should move me emotionally. I may smile at a character or frown or cry, but I am touched in some way. A story line may seem familiar but in this book that I am reading, it has a freshness in its presentation that makes it seem new and original.

I want characters whom I remember long after details of plot have slipped away.

I want a writer who has something to say about life and living life. The theme, like a plot, may be familiar but it is worth hearing again. I take a thought away with me after I close the book, and that thought comes back to me later, some idea worthy of remembrance.

I like books that use literary devices and qualitative language that we can quote when saying that spoken English can be as lyrical as the so-called romance languages. Children have some favorites that bore me to distraction and those they find on their own without my help.

However, when I teach children's literature to adult students, I choose to mention only those books that I find entertaining. If they're good enough for children, they should be good enough for me.

MATT BERMAN

Matt Berman is a third-grade teacher at Metairie Park Country Day School in New Orleans and reviews children's books for The Times-Picayune *and* Kirkus Reviews.

Primarily, teachers look for three things: books which our students will love, books we love as well, and books which have literary merit. This is not as impossible as it sounds. Most of the best children's literature is just as enjoyable to an adult as it is to a child, and a great deal of the best literature published today is sold as children's books.

Determining what students will enjoy is mostly a matter of experience, but there are some basic guidelines. Although children like humor — and if it is not moronic, we like it, too — what they really love is intense emotion. A glance at the all-time favorite books of children bears this out; at the head of the list is *Where the Red Fern Grows*, by Wilson Rawls. Kids like novels that are moving and powerful, that are filled with excitement and tension and a sense of wonder. They like good villains, but they always need a character with whom they can identify, either to be like, or to imagine as a friend. They appreciate being treated as intelligent beings. Finally, they need books which give them lots to think about and daydream about, which spur their imagination.

Within children's literature there is a continuum, from books only children like to books only adults like. The former have no literary merit, and thus don't interest us. They are mostly trash, the characters don't grow, no one learns anything, and they have poor values. The problem with the genre, aside from lack of literary merit, is that kids need more than just having their feelings validated; they need to see that improvement and growth are possible. Just because other kids have the same problems doesn't mean they shouldn't try to improve. They can be better. Books in the middle of the continuum are best for the classroom.

Next, we look for the basic elements of great literature: riveting plots, good characters, powerful emotion, humor, rich vocabulary, detailed description, good values, intellectual depth and generally absorbing reading. It is a myth that kids don't like detailed description. They just have good literary taste; they don't like description that is overblown, overused, vague, unnecessary, airy-fairy, show-offy, or that interferes with, rather than enhances, the movement of the story. Another element, which is helpful but not essential, is an opening hook followed by an exciting first chapter. Probably the most extreme example of this is the first chapter of *A Day No Pigs Would Die*, by Robert Newton Peck.

Finally, we look for books we love. To be successful as teachers, we need to convey to our students our own love of reading and literature. The best children's authors know this, and manage to perform the tricky and miraculous balancing act of writing for a dual audience with little in common but a love of story.

RICHARD PECK

Richard Peck is the popular author of numerous young adult novels. His latest book is for teachers and librarians, Love and Death at the Mall: Teaching and Writing for the Literate Young *from Delacorte.*

To me, a book for a young reader is always a step one young person takes nearer maturity. In my books, that almost always involves distancing the self from the peer group in order to have that first independent thought. American young people already know how to declare their independence from their parents. They need a literature to deliver meaning from their peers.

MEB NORTON

Meb Norton, director of libraries at Metairie Park Country Day School, has spent more than twenty years working with children and books as a storyteller, librarian and parent.

I look for an intangible something that appeals to me and emotionally rings true. I don't distinguish between adult books and children's books while I am reading. When I am finished, I make the link between the book and the child. Some books work well with large classes, others are for the individual.

MARIGNY DUPUY

Marigny Dupuy is a columnist for The Times-Picayune, *writing about children's picture books. Formerly she managed a children's bookstore and studied children's literature at Simmons.*

You would think that a children's bookseller and a reviewer of children's books would be looking for just the same thing in a book, but I have found this to be not necessarily the case.

As a children's bookseller, I cared very much whether a book for children was well written and wonderfully illustrated, but I cared just as much how my young customers and their parents responded to the books. Many times the children were left cold by books I considered spectacularly illustrated and quite well written. Conversely, I found the children sometimes to be utterly devoted to books that I found either too busy or unattractive, or flat and rather dull.

Now I write a monthly column for the newspaper in which I review the latest children's books, and find that my perspective is different: more critical, less commercial. As a reviewer, I consider first the success of the writing and the illustrating on their own, and only then consider the appeal the book will have for children. The very best books have both. Classics such as *The Tale of Peter Rabbit* and *Where the Wild Things Are* and contemporary winners such as *Mirette on the Highwire* and *Grandfather's Journey* are technically nearly perfect. But more importantly, they have an emotional truth and resonance in both the art and the writing that speaks to many people, often adults as well as children.

Elizabeth Robeau Amoss

Elizabeth Robeau Amoss taught sixth- and seventh-grade English at Newman School for twelve years and is now the mother of a two-year-old boy.

Stuck in the children's museum lobby one summer morning, my two-year-old announced to everyone, "Tut, tut, it raining." It wasn't the first time he quoted Milne. From children's books I expect children to learn and adults to be reminded of something enchanting that we can take with us into the real world. As an English teacher I tried to reinforce other subject matter with my selections. Books rich in metaphor, imagery, and irony — typical sixth-grade fare — best lend themselves to being read aloud. For my son, I look for books that rely on language as their primary method of character development. I want to give him words.

Kevin McCaffrey

Kevin McCaffrey has been in the children's book business for nineteen years. He is president of The Children's Hour, a children's book emporium, and of Booksellers, Inc., books at wholesale and for book fairs. He has served on the Board of American Booksellers Association and founded New Orleans-Gulf South Booksellers Association.

It's hard to pinpoint what goes into buying books for resale. It starts with your own basic tastes and knowing the tastes of many friends and customers, that is, the ones you respect and trust. Then there are basic rules you go by. For instance, I like a little story with my morals, so I never respond to something too overt concerning morals. I like the moral to work on you long after you've read the story. I like a story with layers. I like a story with characters who act and respond in a real kind of way.

When it comes to art, I respond to many different forms and techniques. This comes from my background in art as well as my interest in researching and viewing many contemporary cutting-edge styles. I like art that is well done for whatever esthetic reasons I relate to. If that is too vague then, specifically, I also respond to art appropriate to the book design, and if it helps further the overall effect of the story, much like film tries to weave a mesmerizingly seamless web of story, characterization and visuals.

Finally, I consider books in three categories. Children's books are for libraries, book-fair sales or retail store sales. Library books can be a bit more straight and informational. Book-fair books must have the ability to leap off the table into the buyer's hands by magic (and the jacket). They somehow must recommend themselves. Bookstore books can be hand sold and recommended by the store workers. They are good books that might otherwise sit quietly on the shelf, but get passed on and sold through love.

Berthe Amoss

Over the years, my taste in children's books has evolved, and I have chosen books for various reasons. As a child, I loved book illustrations, especially those of Tenniel, H.J. Ford, Edmund Dulac, Arthur Rackham and Maxfield Parrish. My favorite books were all of Andrew Lang's fairy tale collections, the Oz books, Nancy Drew books, and *Heidi*.

In the sixties, when I was trying to get published, I looked for books that I wished I could have written or illustrated. Among my favorite illustrators were Edward Ardizzone, Maurice Sendak, Arnold Lobel and Irene Haas. The writers I admired most were Eleanor Farjeon, Eleanor Cameron, Richard Peck, E.L. Konigsburg and Mary Stolz, to name only a few, because the list is endless.

In the eighties, when I was writing a column for *The Times-Picayune* and teaching children's literature at Tulane, I looked for books with illustrations that could qualify as fine art, such as those of Innocenti and Van Allsburg, and authors whose writing skills outshone their "message," writers such as Isaac Bashevis Singer, E.B. White and Randall Jarrell. I had the naive hope that I could convince the English department that children's literature belonged to English literature.

Now, with only myself to please, I have become a bookaholic. If I see a book I like, I want to own it. I notice everything about a book: the paper, the design, the binding, the quality of the printing, and, of course, the text and the illustrations. For me, the picture book is an art form, visually exciting and emotionally rewarding to be studied and enjoyed many times over, and the best YA's are as fulfilling as the best adult fiction.

Eric Suben

Garth Williams's *The Chicken Book* is a good example of what I look for in a children's book. This simple picture book appears to be nothing more than a silly rhyme about five chicks and a mother hen. But the book communicates on a variety of levels, beginning with a lesson on what chickens eat and an exercise in counting to five. The artist's characteristically gorgeous pictures provide a wealth of information about life in a barnyard and a guessing game that lets the small child "outsmart" the chicks by spotting the desired morsel before the chick can find it. Finally, the book has the overarching theme of a parent's love, shown by her providing for and teaching her children.

All books should be similarly rich with meaning and full of life. Henry David Thoreau wrote that "a truly good book is something as natural, and as unexpectedly and unaccountably fair and perfect, as a wildflower." I, like Thoreau, seek something unexpected and natural. Strong, interesting, realistic characters will always do or say something you don't expect, something *real*. Look at Tom Sawyer, Jo March, Heidi, Dorothy Gale, Ramona Quimby. In picture books, look at *Harold and the Purple Crayon*. The life in these books — the thing that keeps us turning the pages — is the reality and charm of people coming through all kinds of experiences with their humanity and individuality intact. That is the best example we can provide for children and the most important thing we can show in books. And the book doesn't have to be complex to do it. The palpable goodness of the mother in *The Chicken Book*, a doggerel rhyme of just over one hundred words, transcends the simplicity of the medium and lives in readers' hearts.

MOSTLY CLASSICS AND FAVORITE PICTURE BOOKS

BY MARIGNY DUPUY

1. Goodnight Moon *by Margaret Wise Brown, illus. by Clement Hurd*
2. Pat the Bunny *by Dorothy Kunhardt*
3. Little Fur Family *by Margaret Wise Brown, illus. by Garth Williams*
4. Max's Ride *by Rosemary Wells*
5. Max's First Word *by Rosemary Wells*
6. Where's Spot *by Eric Hill*
7. Blueberries for Sal *by Robert McCloskey*
8. Make Way for Ducklings *by Robert McCloskey*
9. Caps for Sale *by Esphyr Slobodkina*
10. Millions of Cats *by Wanda Gág*
11. Cat in the Hat *by Dr. Seuss*
12. Corduroy *by Donald Freeman*
13. Curious George *by H. A. Rey*
14. Drummer Hoff *by Barbara Emberley, illus. by Ed Emberley*
15. Each Peach Pear Plum *by Janet & Allan Ahlberg*
16. Frederick *by Leo Lionni*
17. George Shrinks *by William Joyce*
18. I Am a Bunny *by Ole Risom, illus. by Richard Scarry*
19. If You Give a Mouse a Cookie *by Laura Numeroff, illus. by Felicia Bond*
20. Jesse Bear, What Will You Wear? *by Nancy White Carlstrom, illus. by Bruce Degen*
21. Madeline *by Ludwig Bemelmans*
22. Madeline's Rescue *by Ludwig Bemelmans*
23. Strega Nona *by Tomie DePaola*
24. May I Bring A Friend? *by Beatrice Schenk deRegniers, illus. by Beni Montresor*
25. Where the Wild Things Are *by Maurice Sendak*
26. The Nutshell Library *by Maurice Sendak*
27. Ira Sleeps Over *by Bernard Waber*
28. Swimmy *by Leo Lionni*
29. Fish is Fish *by Leo Lionni*
30. The Very Hungry Caterpillar *by Eric Carle*
31. Mother, Mother, I Want Another *by Maria Poluskin, illus. by Diane Dawson*
32. Mr. Gumpy's Outing *by John Burningham*
33. The Napping House *by Don & Audrey Wood*
34. Heckedy Peg *by Don & Audrey Wood*
35. Peter's Chair *by Ezra Jack Keats*
36. One Fish, Two Fish, Red Fish, Blue Fish *by Dr. Seuss*
37. Are You My Mother? *by P. D. Eastman*
38. The Little House *by Virginia Burton*
39. The Real Mother Goose
40. The Runaway Bunny *by Margaret Wise Brown, illus. by Clement Hurd*
41. Stone Soup *by Marcia Brown*
42. Story of Ferdinand *by Munro Leaf, illus. by Robert Lawson*
43. The Tale of Peter Rabbit *by Beatrix Potter*
44. Ten, Nine, Eight *by Molly Bang*
45. Tikki, Tikki, Tembo *by Arlene Mosel, illus. by Blair Lent*

MATT BERMAN'S FAVORITE CHAPTER BOOKS AND YOUNG ADULT NOVELS

GENERALLY GREAT BOOKS

Steal Away
Jennifer Armstrong
   In 1855 two thirteen-year-old girls, one white, one black, run away from a southern farm and make the difficult journey north to freedom, living to recount their story forty-one years later to two similar young girls.

Sounder
William H. Armstrong
   Newbery Medal 1970. Angry and humiliated when his sharecropper father is jailed for stealing food, a young black boy grows in courage and understanding by learning to read and with the help of his devoted dog, Sounder.

The Indian in the Cupboard
Lynne Reid Banks
   Book 1 of the Indian series. A nine-year-old boy receives a plastic Indian, a cupboard and a little key for his birthday and finds himself involved in adventure when the Indian comes to life in the cupboard and befriends him.

On My Honor
Marion Dane Bauer
   Newbery Honor 1987. When his best friend drowns while they are both swimming in a treacherous river that they had promised never to go near, Joel is devastated and terrified of having to tell both sets of parents the terrible consequences of their disobedience.

A Gathering of Days
Joan W. Blos
   Newbery Medal 1980. The journal of a fourteen-year-old girl, kept the last years she lived on the family farm, records daily events in her small New Hampshire town, her father's remarriage, and the death of her own best friend.

Dandelion Wine
Ray Bradbury
   In a small town in 1928, a twelve-year-old boy savors the magic of childhood and the wonders of summer.

The Return of the Twelves
Pauline Clarke
    Max finds twelve old wooden soldiers in the attic of his home and discovers they are alive. Historians have long been looking for them, since they belonged to the Brontës, and, if found, they might be sold to an American museum where Max would never see them again.

The Winchesters
James Lincoln Collier
    Fourteen-year-old Chris, a poor relation of the wealthy Winchesters, must choose to be on the side of management or labor when his classmates' parents go on strike at the Winchester mill in response to a wage cut.

James and the Giant Peach
Roald Dahl
    Wonderful adventures abound after James escapes from his fearful aunts by rolling away inside a giant peach.

Weasel
Cynthia DeFelice
    Alone in the frontier wilderness in the winter of 1839 while his father is recovering from an injury, eleven-year-old Nathan runs afoul of the renegade killer known as Weasel and makes a surprising discovery about the concept of revenge.

Indian at Hawk's Hill
Allan A. Eckert
    Newbery Honor 1972. A shy, lonely six-year-old wanders into the Canadian prairie and spends a summer under the protection of a badger.

Momo
Michael Ende
    Momo discovers a plot by the men in gray to steal everybody's time.

The Neverending Story
Michael Ende
    The magic tale of Bastian, a lonely, solitary boy who steps through the pages of a book into a special kingdom where he learns the true measure of his courage and creates a new world with his wishes.

The Slave Dancer
Paula Fox
    Newbery Medal 1974. Kidnapped by the crew of an Africa-bound ship, a thirteen-year-old boy discovers to his horror that he is on a slaver and his job is to play music for the exercise periods of the human cargo.

Stone Fox
John R. Gardiner
    Little Willie hopes to pay back taxes on his grandfather's farm with the purse from a dog sled race he enters.

A Dig in Time
Peni R. Griffin

 While spending the summer with their grandmother in San Antonio, twelve-year-old Nan and her younger brother find artifacts buried in the yard and discover how to use them to travel back through time to significant moments in their family history.

The Planet of Junior Brown
Virginia Hamilton

 Newbery Honor 1972. Already a leader in New York's underground world of homeless children, Buddy Clark takes on the responsibility of protecting the overweight, emotionally disturbed friend with whom he has been playing hooky from eighth grade all semester.

North to Freedom
Anne Holm

 Having escaped from an Eastern European concentration camp where he has spent his life, a twelve-year-old boy struggles to cope with an entirely strange world as he flees northward to freedom in Denmark.

Slake's Limbo
Felice Holman

 Thirteen-year-old Aremis Slake, hounded by his fears and misfortunes, flees into New York City's subway tunnels, never again, he believes, to emerge.

The Lottery Rose
Irene Hunt

 A young victim of child abuse gradually overcomes his fears and suspicions when placed in a home with other boys.

The Phantom Tollbooth
Norton Juster

 A journey through the land where Milo learns the importance of words and numbers provides a cure for his boredom.

Father's Arcane Daughter
E.L. Konigsburg

 Kidnapped seventeen years before, a man's daughter by a former marriage appears at his new home in Pittsburg and affects the entire family.

King Matt the First
Janusz Korczak

 A child king introduces reforms to give children the same rights as adults.

To Kill a Mockingbird
Harper Lee

 Eight-year-old Scout Finch tells of life in a small Alabama town where her father is a lawyer, and where she and her brother are thrust into an adult world of racial bigotry and hatred when their father chooses to defend a black man charged with raping a white girl.

Unclaimed Treasures
Patricia MacLachlan
   Willa, who wants to feel extraordinary, thinks that she's in love with the father of the boy next door until she realizes that her ordinary true love is the boy himself.

Goodnight, Mr. Tom
Michelle Magorian
   A battered child learns to embrace life when he is adopted by an old man in the English countryside during the Second World War.

Bridge to Terabithia
Katherine Paterson
   Newbery Medal 1978. The life of a 10-year-old boy in rural Virginia expands when be becomes friends with a newcomer who subsequently meets an untimely death when she tries to reach their hideaway, Terabithia, during a storm.

Hatchet
Gary Paulsen
   Newbery Honor 1988. After a plane crash, thirteen-year-old Brian spends fifty-four days in the wilderness, learning to survive with only the aid of a hatchet given to him by his mother, and learning also to survive his parents' divorce.

The Boy Who Could Make Himself Disappear
Kin Platt
   A twelve-year-old boy with a psychological speech defect gradually develops a schizophrenic withdrawal after moving from Los Angeles to live with his mother in New York following the divorce of his harsh and detached parents.

Truckers
Terry Pratchet
   First book of *The Bromeliad*. Reluctant to believe that there's a world outside the department store where they live, the Nomes look to Masklin, a newly arrived "outsider", to lead them to a safe haven when the store goes out of business.

Where the Red Fern Grows
Wilson Rawls
   The adventures of a ten-year-old boy and the two dogs he bought with the money he earned.

The Light in the Forest
Conrad Richter
   After being raised an Indian for eleven years following his capture at the age of four, John Butler is forcibly returned to his white parents but continues to long for the freedom of Indian life.

A Fine White Dust
Cynthia Rylant
   Newbery Honor 1987. The visit of the traveling Preacher Man to his small North Carolina town gives new impetus to thirteen-year-old Peter's struggle to reconcile his own deeply felt religious belief with the beliefs and non-beliefs of his family and friends.

There's a Boy in the Girls' Bathroom
Louis Sachar

     An unmanageable but lovable eleven-year-old misfit learns to believe in himself when he gets to know the new school counselor, who is sort of a misfit, too.

The Bears' House
Marilyn Sachs

     Fran Ellen is ostracized by her class because she sucks her thumb and smells bad, but her dreadful home life is a secret she tries to keep from them all.

Words by Heart
Ouida Sebestyen

     A young black girl struggles to fulfill her papa's dream of a better future for their family in the Southwestern town where, in 1910, they are the only blacks.

The Eyes of Kid Midas
Neil Shusterman

     Kevin is entranced when he finds a pair of sunglasses that turn his desires into reality, but things start to get out of control.

A Tree Grows in Brooklyn
Betty Smith

     Young Francie Nolan experiences the problems of growing up in a Brooklyn, New York, slum.

Maniac Magee
Jerry Spinelli

     Newbery Medal 1991. After his parents die, Jerry Lionel Magee's life becomes legendary after he accomplishes athletic and other feats that awe his contemporaries.

The Cay
Theodore Taylor

     When the freighter on which they are traveling is torpedoed by a German submarine during World War II, an adolescent white boy, blinded by a blow on the head, and an old black man are stranded on a tiny Caribbean island where the boy acquires a new kind of vision, courage, and love from his old companion.

A Child's Christmas in Wales
Dylan Thomas

     A Welsh poet recalls the celebration of Christmas in Wales and the feelings it evoked in him as a child.

UNUSUAL THEMES

Nothing but the Truth
Avi

     Newbery Honor 1992. A ninth grader's suspension for singing "The Star Spangled Banner" during homeroom becomes a national news story.

Tuck Everlasting
Natalie Babbitt
    The Tuck family is confronted with an agonizing situation when they discover that a ten-year-old girl and a malicious stranger now share their secret about a spring whose water prevents one from ever growing older.

The Secret Garden
Frances Hodgson Burnett
    A boy who has lived as a spoiled invalid regains his health when he and his orphaned cousin restore a once-lovely garden.

The Chocolate War
Robert Cormier
    PG Language. A high school freshman discovers the devastating consequences of refusing to join the school's annual fund-raising drive and arousing the wrath of the school bullies.

Tunes for Bears to Dance to
Robert Cormier
    Eleven-year-old Henry escapes his family's problems by watching the wood carving of Mr. Levine, an elderly Holocaust survivor, but when Henry is manipulated into betraying his friend, he comes to know true evil.

A Bone From a Dry Sea
Peter Dickinson
    In two parallel stories, an intelligent female of a prehistoric tribe becomes instrumental in advancing the lot of her people, and the daughter of a paleontologist visits Africa when important fossil remains are discovered.

Lord of the Flies
William Golding
    Stranded on an island while an atomic war destroys the rest of the world, a group of young boys revert to savagery as they struggle to survive.

Shoebag
Mary James
    Shoebag, a happy cockroach who finds himself suddenly changed into a little boy, changes the lives of those around him before returning to his former life as an insect.

The Battle Horse
Harry Kullman
    The children on a Stockholm street engage in a modern-day jousting tournament in which the rich are knights and the poor are horses who bear them.

In the Year of the Boar and Jackie Robinson
Betty Bao Lord
    In 1947, a Chinese child comes to Brooklyn where she becomes Americanized at school, in her apartment building, and by her love for baseball.

The Giver
Lois Lowry
　　Newbery Medal 1994. Given his lifetime assignment at the Ceremony of Twelve, Jonas becomes the receiver of memories shared by only one other in his community and discovers the terrible truth about the society in which he lives.

Shiloh
Phyllis Reynolds Naylor
　　Newbery Medal 1992. When he finds a lost beagle in the hills behind his West Virginia home, Marty tries to hide it from his family and the dog's real owner, a mean-spirited man known to shoot deer out of season and to mistreat his dogs.

Unusual Settings

One More River
Lynne Reid Banks
　　Fourteen-year-old Lesley is upset when her parents abandon their comfortable life in Canada for a kibbutz in Israel prior to the 1967 war.

Face to Face
Marion Dane Bauer
　　Picked on by the school bullies, thirteen-year-old Michael confronts his fears during a trip to Colorado to see his father, who works as a whitewater rafting guide and whom Michael has not seen in eight years.

Where the Lillies Bloom
Vera and Bill Cleaver
　　In the Great Smoky Mountains, a fourteen-year-old girl struggles to keep her family together after her father dies.

AK
Peter Dickinson
　　When a military coup occurs in the constantly war torn African country of Nagala, teenage Paul is forced to flee into the open countryside to avoid enemy soldiers who seek his life.

Julie of the Wolves
Jean Craighead George
　　Newbery Medal 1973. While running away from home and an unwanted marriage, a thirteen-year-old Eskimo girl becomes lost on the North Slope of Alaska and befriended by a wolf pack.

From the Mixed Up Files of Mrs. Basil E. Frankweiler
E.L. Konigsburg
　　Newbery Medal 1968. Two suburban children run away from their Connecticut home and go to New York's Metropolitan Museum of Art, where their ingenuity enables them to live in luxury.

Island of the Blue Dolphins
Scott O'Dell

   Newbery Medal 1961. An Indian girl lives alone for eighteen years on an isolated island off the California coast where her tribe emigrated and she was left behind.

A Day No Pigs Would Die
Robert Newton Peck

   To a thirteen-year-old Vermont farm boy whose father slaughters pigs for a living, maturity comes early as he learns doing what's got to be done, especially regarding his pet pig who cannot produce a litter.

The Yearling
Marjorie Kinnan Rawlings

   A young boy living in the Florida backwoods is forced to decide the fate of a fawn he has lovingly raised as a pet.

Call It Courage
Armstrong Sperry

   Newbery Medal 1941. Based on a Polynesian legend, this is the story of a youth, who, though afraid of the sea, sets out alone in his canoe to conquer his fear and prove his courage to himself and his tribe.

Taste of Salt
Francis Temple

   In the hospital after being beaten by Macoutes, seventeen-year-old Djo tells the story of his impoverished life to a young woman who, like him, has been working with the social reformer Father Aristide to fight the repression in Haiti.

The Emperor's Winding Sheet
Jill Paton Walsh

   An English boy, shipwrecked, hungry, and lost, finds his way into the court of Constantine where he is interpreted as the symbol of good luck and, as such, ordered to be kept always near the king.

MAKING EVERY WORD COUNT

The Shoeshine Girl
Clyde Robert Bulla

   Determined to earn some money, ten-year-old Sarah Ida gets a job at a shoeshine stand and learns a great many things besides shining shoes.

The Children's Story
James Clavell

   A new teacher uses charm and fallacious logic to brainwash a class of second graders after the U.S. has been conquered by an enemy nation.

Sadako and the Thousand Paper Cranes
Eleanor Coeri

Hospitalized with the dreaded disease leukemia, a child in Hiroshima races against time to fold 1,000 paper cranes to verify the legend that by doing so a sick person will become healthy.

Morning Girl
Michael Dorris

Morning Girl, who loves the day, and her younger brother, who loves the night, take turns describing their life on a island in pre-Columbian America.

The Hundred Dresses
Eleanor Estes

Newbery Honor 1945. In winning a medal she is no longer there to receive, a tight-lipped little Polish girl teaches her classmates a lesson.

Sarah, Plain and Tall
Patricia MacLachlan

Newbery Medal 1986. When their father invites a mail-order bride to come live with them in their prairie home, Caleb and Anna are captivated by their new mother and hope that she will stay.

Through Grandpa's Eyes
Patricia MacLachlan

A young boy learns a different way of seeing the world from his blind grandfather.

Stargone John
Ellen Kindt McKenzie

Six-year-old John, emotionally withdrawn and resistant to traditional teaching methods, experiences ridicule and punishment at his one-room school-house, until an old retired teacher reaches out from her blindness to share with him the world of reading and writing.

Annie and the Old One
Miska Miles

Newbery Honor 1972. A Navajo girl unravels a day's weaving on a rug whose completion, she believes, will mean the death of her Grandmother.

Mississippi Bridge
Mildred Taylor

During a heavy rainstorm in 1930s rural Mississippi, a ten-year-old white boy sees a bus driver order all black passengers off a crowded bus to make room for late-arriving white passengers and then set off across the raging Rosa Lee Creek.

STRONG CHARACTERS

The True Confessions of Charlotte Doyle
by Avi

   Newbery Honor 1991. As the lone young lady on a transatlantic voyage in 1832, Charlotte learns that the captain is murderous and the crew rebellious.

The Moves Make the Man
Bruce Brooks

   Newbery Honor 1985. A black boy and an emotionally troubled white boy in North Carolina form a precarious friendship.

What Hearts
Bruce Brooks

   Newbery Honor 1993. After his mother divorces his father and remarries, Asa's sharp intellect and capacity for forgiveness help him deal with the instabilities of his new world.

Ramona the Pest
Beverly Cleary

   Ramona is a little sister who always wants to tag along after Beezus and the older kids.

Hazel Rye
Vera and Bill Cleaver

   An eleven-year-old girl with no appreciation for land and growing things finds her values beginning to change when she agrees to let an impoverished family live in a small house she owns.

Thursday's Children
Rumer Godden

   As he tags along to his spoiled sister's ballet classes, Doone discovers and develops his own rare and special talents.

Quest for a Maid
Frances Mary Hendry

   Aware of her sister's deadly efforts to secure the Scottish throne for Robert de Brus, Meg realizes she must protect the young Norwegian princess who has been chosen as rightful heir.

George
E.L. Kongisburg

   When twelve-year-old Benjamin refuses to see what is going on in his chemistry lab, the little man who lives inside of him must finally speak out in public for the safety of all concerned.

Afternoon of the Elves
Janet Taylor Lisle

Newbery Honor 1990. As Hillary works in the miniature village allegedly built by elves in Sara-Kate's backyard, she becomes more and more curious about Sara-Kate's real life inside her big house with her mysterious mother.

The Facts and Fictions of Minna Pratt
Patricia MacLachlan

An eleven-year-old cellist learns about life from her eccentric family, her first boyfriend, and Mozart.

The Ghost Belonged to Me
Richard Peck

In 1913 in the Midwest, a quartet of characters share adventures from exploding steamboats to exorcizing a ghost.

Bless the Beasts and Children
Glendon Swarthout

While at Box Canyon Boys Camp, several disturbed boys search for a way to improve their lives.

Lost Magic
Berthe Amoss

In the Middle Ages, orphaned Ceridwen learns the art of herbal healing and gains the protection of the local lord until she is accused of witchcraft.